Breaking My Silence

Janie at the Copa in New York, 1968

Breaking My Silence

Confessions of a Rat Pack Party Girl
and Sex-trade Survivor

Jane McCormick

with

Patti Wicklund

St. Paul • Rapfire Press • 2007

Rapfire Press
P.O. Box 270245
St. Paul, MN 55127
651-286-9817

Website: www.breakingmysilence.net
ISBN 978-1-60461-477-0
Library of Congress Control Number: 2007936577
Manufactured in United States of America

Cover art and design: Patti Wicklund
Editing, text design, production: E. B. Green Editorial, St. Paul
Indexing: Patricia Green, Homer, Alaska

To all the sisters still out there

Preface

One morning, about fifteen years ago, I realized that whenever I was with friends, or even talking with a stranger, the conversation inevitably turned to some crazy, zany, tragic event in my life. Listeners seemed to find my anecdotes amazing; many said, "Janie, you should write a book." After all my then-almost-fifty years, however, I felt I must do more than tell stories. I had something to say to men and women, especially those used, battered, and abused.

I didn't have time then, but after being disabled in an industrial accident, I grabbed a tablet and just let it flow—words, ideas, random thoughts. In a few months I filled several spiral notebooks and put them in a drawer of my old brown filing cabinet, waiting for the day they would become sentences and paragraphs, pages and chapters.

On my fiftieth birthday, I bought a tape recorder and went to Las Vegas; I would tell my stories to the recorder and find someone to help me write. I wanted my story to be compelling, one that women and girls might learn from and so find help and hope for their own lives.

I knew many who had suffered their own versions of trauma, molestation, and abuse. Perhaps my story could give them the strength to survive; perhaps it could give younger women information that would help them decide not to enter prostitution, show them that getting out is way harder than getting in.

The law frowns on prostitutes but doesn't consider the reasons that women have turned to this profession or that they may not have chosen it at all. Nine times out of ten, a man is in the picture, promising money, promising love. If I had my way, the pimps who suck the lifeblood from and chain women to a life of abuse would pay. And to all the johns, I'd say, "Stay home with your wives. If you don't buy sex, no one will sell it." (See Epilogue & Resources for more on this topic.)

This work is not intended to hurt anyone (a few names have been changed or not provided to protect privacy) but to tell the truth about prostitution, what got me there, and how I started to get out. I have pictured the players as clearly as I can remember. Some were wonderful and crazy; others not. Some are still part of my life; others have passed on to other places and dimensions.

My deepfelt thanks to all those who have supported me in this "literary" endeavor—especially Patti Wicklund. This book would not exist without her.

—Jane McCormick

1

I was running for my life. I jumped out of the cab, tossed a twenty at the driver, and ran—hoping no one followed, hoping that if he did, he couldn't see me—through the lobby to the ticket counter. I pushed in front, demanded a ticket on the next flight to Orange County, and slapped down the fare in cash.

"Three minutes to get to the plane," she said.

"Good!" I headed for the gate. Gulping for air, my heart pounding, I ran. Someone was behind me, running too. Was he still after me? I was too scared to slow down, too scared to look.

Keep going . . . just keep going! I felt sick to my stomach; a pain wrenched my side. There was no one at the gate. I pushed through the door and ran out on the tarmac as fast as my high-heels could carry me. Someone who looked like a mechanic was rolling the portable stairs from the plane.

"Wait! Please help me!" I shouted.

He rolled the stairs back; I clambered up, was just to the top when

I heard the door from the terminal slam open: "Janie!"

I didn't look back. The stewardess looked at my ticket and pointed to an empty seat. I sat down next to the window and fastened my seatbelt. I felt like I was going to throw up.

"Take off. Take off," I prayed, closing my eyes, hoping the stairs wouldn't be pulled up again. Mercifully, the engine revved, and the plane started to roll. I was safe! At least for the moment. I hoped I'd be safe at my mother's, too.

Once the plane was in the air, I tried to collect myself. I looked down at the skirt of my thousand-dollar suit. I had $800 in cash in my handbag, but I'd left everything else—cars, money, clothes, jewelry, fur coats, a home—behind. I'd earned it all by hustling, and by being hustled, in Vegas.

I was only beginning to step back far enough to see that my life had gone horribly wrong. I would have to change it even to survive. How did I get here? How did I arrive at *this* day and this run for my life? I'd have to go back to the beginning . . .

2

I was born on March 29, 1941, in a Marion, Indiana, hospital room barely large enough for three patients. Long, white cotton drapes divided three stations equipped with forceps, scalpel, and needles. Cigarette smoke filled the waiting room, where fathers paced the floor and family members played penny-ante poker.

They could hear the screams of every delivering mother, the nurse's gentle encouraging voice, "Take deep a breath . . . and push . . . " until the newborn's cry announced entry to the world. The father beamed; the family praised the new arrival.

Wilma Frances McCormick ("Mickey," my mother) was in the middle bed. She had been in labor for twenty hours while the other two beds revolved patients like slot machines.

"This baby must be a girl. My son never gave me this much trouble," Mickey told the nurse.

Dr. James Allan was a strikingly handsome man in his late twenties, dressed in a white, half-buttoned doctor's coat with a stethoscope dangling from his neck. He shuffled smoothly between the first and third stations, delivering orders and babies. Sweat poured from his forehead as he stopped to check Mickey's dilation.

"How are you doing, Mickey?" Dr. Allan asked.

She shook her head with frustration and said, "I wish this baby would hurry up and come out, so I can get back to living my life."

Doctor Allan rose from the stool at the end of the bed, put his hand on her tummy, and said, "This little baby is breech, wants to come out feet first. That's why you're in so much trouble. I'm going to talk to your husband."

Dr. Allan walked through the drawn curtain and signaled Oren McCormick ("Bus," my father) to follow him.

Bus, of Irish heritage, was dressed in blue work clothes, a Coca-Cola logo sewn on the chest of his shirt. He was six feet tall, of slender build, and had copper-toned skin, dark brown hair, an oblong face accented by high cheekbones, and a set of dreamy, hazel eyes. He followed the doctor into a separate room.

"What's wrong, Dr. Allan? My poor wife can't take much more!"

Dr. Allan explained, "This is a dangerous situation, and I need you to make a life decision. Bus, you have to understand, if this baby doesn't turn around, I may have to open her up, and if I have to do that . . . I'll only have time to save one life. If it comes down to that, which life do you want me to save—your wife's or the baby's?"

Bus stared at the wall in disbelief. Dr. Allan grabbed his arm, awaiting the decision.

Suddenly, I kicked Mom hard (so I'm told) and she screamed, shaking the room. The nurse shouted, "Doctor, the baby is coming!"

Dr. Allan rushed to her side, and like a raging bull, I kicked myself out, feet first, ripping my mother apart. The doctor untangled the umbilical cord from my neck, cleared the airway, held me upside down by my feet, and slapped my backside. Lungs filled, I bellowed a long, high-pitched cry. Then silence, as everyone turned to see who I was.

Dr. Allan laughed as he held me up and said, "Mickey, you have a heroic, blond baby girl with the kick of a swimmer and the vocal cords of an opera star." My father almost burst with relief, and the God-loving McCormick family hooped and hollered. Mom was in pain but spurted again, "She had to be a girl. Dick never gave me that much trouble when he was born." And with her next breath, "I'm going to call her Jane Etta. Like Dick and Jane from the reading book."

My mother, a single child, had grown up in Jonesboro, Indiana, twenty-five miles south of Marion. She had the personality of a show-girl. Her makeup, hair, nails, and clothes were of top priority. She had a beautiful build, a gorgeous face, and a quick, witty approach to life. Outgoing and in your face, she was always willing to speak her mind. And she was always ready to dance in her size fours.

Mom loved to play the piano and get the tavern hopping. Once she had a few cocktails, she would fold her body up like a pretzel and walk across the bar on her butt. "You know . . . I don't smoke, I don't drink, and I don't curse," she'd say and pretend to look for something on the table: "Dammit. I left my cigarettes in the beer joint."

Mom told me as I was growing up that I kept her from being with the "real man" she wanted all her life. I never knew who that "real man" was—she seemed to need two or three men to make her feel okay. Mom liked to attract men, and she flaunted herself before them all; then she teased them with her barroom bump-and-grind.

My father grew up on a farm thirty miles east of Marion in Peru, Indiana, with my grandparents and Uncle Jimmy. Father was a hard-working family man; his personality was totally opposite that of my mother. He was calm, quiet, caring, and deeply in love with her.

My parents rented a twenty-acre spread of land near Logansport, Indiana. We lived in a two-story farmhouse that had a kitchen with a pump for running well water, a wood-burning stove for cooking and heating the house. The living room was next to the kitchen, and a steep set of stairs led to the two bedrooms on the second floor.

Each morning at sunrise, Dad jumped up with the rooster's crow. He planted the land with sweet corn and tasty tomatoes. The barn and farmyard bustled with dairy cows and squealing pigs, and in the hen-house the chickens were busy dropping eggs into their nests. After my father finished feeding the farm animals and tending the cornfields, he went into Logansport to drive a Coca-Cola truck to make an extra buck. Mom hated being alone in the country.

On December 7, 1941, the Japanese bombed Pearl Harbor. The United States entered World War II in full swing, and many of the local men were drafted into service, leaving their wives and families to work the farms. Two years later on one particular Sunday after church, Mom met another man. He was a clean-cut, stocky ex-marine with a fancy car and a suave manner. She invited him to the farm to help with the chores. That same week, after my father left for work, the ex-marine showed up at the front door, looking sharp and smelling really good. A few months later, Mom asked my father for a divorce. It was final on December 27, 1943. Father joined the army, and the court ordered him to pay child support of forty dollars per month.

In January 1944 I was three and my brother, Dick, a skinny five-year-old. We had no choice but to accept our mother's new husband into our lives. Our stepfather, Woodrow Thomas Allen ("Woody"), was an inactive master sergeant from the U.S. Marine Corps. Mom loved having this strong man around the farm. She fussed with cleaning more than she ever had when she was married to our father. When Woody was around, Mom spent all her time flirting with him. She also seemed to favor Dick over me. I was made to believe that little girls should be seen and not heard.

Woody paid a lot of attention to me when he was alone with me, more than I cared for or ever felt was quite right. I hated taking naps because I was afraid I'd wake up to feel him hovering over me.

One afternoon after Mom had put me down for a nap, Woody came upstairs to my bedroom and started tickling my waist and legs. I tickled and giggled with him. Then he rubbed my little body all over, starting with my arms, then the back and front of my upper body, then my legs, and finally between the front and then the back of my legs. He told me, "Daddy loves you," while he rocked himself against the side of my bed. I was afraid to move, but I thought that was how stepfathers loved their little girls.

When Woody was done, he looked mad and growled, "Now remember Janie, you're my little doll baby, and this is our little secret, because I'll kill you if you tell your mother or brother."

I wondered why what he did made me feel dirty, like something was wrong. Inside, I was always scared. I became so afraid, in fact, that every time I saw Woody I ran to hide.

I knew that Mom loved me . . . and that she didn't do that to me. I knew my brother loved me . . . and he didn't do that either. I didn't understand what love was, but I did know that at night, when I shared the small bedroom with my brother, Woody never bothered me.

One morning Mom told us to go outside and play. Dick and I walked over to the barnyard to watch Woody cleaning the drinking trough for the animals. Woody handed me a metal bucket and asked me to get him some water. I took the bucket and rushed to retrieve water from the well near the house. While I was gone, Woody told my brother he was going to play a little joke on me. He took some jumper cables from the barn and connected the cables to a used car battery and then to the steel trough.

When I returned with the bucket, he told me to pour the water into the trough. I lifted the half-full bucket and began pouring it into the empty trough. As soon as the water hit the metal, I received an electric shock. I screamed and fell to the ground. My body shook, and my hands tingled like a thousand poking pins.

Woody laughed, and then Dick laughed with him.

"Did you see the look on her face when it knocked her down?" Woody asked. "You see, Dick, it didn't kill her; it just stunned her."

Janie, at about age four

Dick jumped off the wooden fence and ran to my side. His eyes narrowed, his smile turned to hate. He helped me to my feet and brushed the sand from my clothes.

I didn't know what had happened. At first I thought the trough had knocked me down, but when I got my wits back, I realized Woody had played a mean trick. I felt he used me to teach Dick a lesson about how to treat girls. I knew Woody wouldn't have done that to Dick.

Woody continued to laugh as he lit a cigarette and pulled a small bottle of whisky from his back pocket. He looked at Dick and said, "I don't know why you're so upset. It's just a joke!"

Then Woody marched up to us, squinted, and in a stern voice said, "I'll spank you both if you tell your Mom about this. This is our little secret, and don't you two forget that."

3

At the end of the farming season in September 1944, Woody and Mom decided to move and start new careers. They packed up our small belongings and drove away.

Dick and I rode in the back seat of the fancy car, listening to the laughter of the two lovebirds in the front seat. Mom was a different kind of woman after she married Woody. The two of them loved to drink and act carefree. Mom made me laugh when one of her favorite songs came on the radio. She reached over, turned the volume to blaring, and sang along at the top of her lungs, encouraging Dick and me to join in.

After driving through the day, we passed a restaurant and house on Highway 65. A sign there read, "For Rent, Help Wanted." Woody stopped the car, and we went in to eat dinner. Afterwards, Woody drove us across the highway to rent a room at a motel.

The room had a double bed with a pullout couch, a lamp on a table, two chairs next to the window, an indoor shower, and a radio. It was nice to have an indoor bathroom with running water—something we never had at the farm.

Later that evening, Woody and Mom walked across the parking lot to the motel tavern. Dick and I stayed in the room and listened to the radio until we fell asleep.

The next morning Woody announced that we were going to run the restaurant there and that we were going to live in the house right next door. The restaurant had a large parking lot in front, where semi-trailers could park and their drivers could sleep overnight.

The attached house was a furnished, one-bedroom home with indoor plumbing. The kitchen and living room were midsized rooms with a small couch, kitchen table, and four chairs. In the back was a large wooded yard. Woody and Mom moved their things into the bedroom, and Dick and I shared the lumpy couch in the living room.

Every day after that the two of them—Mom and Woody—started at 4 a.m. They worked seven days a week for about twelve hours per day. Woody cooked in his checkered pants and white hat and shirt, and Mom served the customers in her little white apron, black skirt, and short-sleeved blouse. I thought she looked so pretty when she went to work. I loved her so much, even if she couldn't protect me from her new husband.

One morning at the kitchen table, Mom said, as she put on her apron for work, "I don't want you two kids playing in the parking lot at the end of the restaurant today. The gypsies' families are here for the state fair, and last night I saw them drinking beer and breaking bottles behind the booths." She grabbed our chins and looked into our eyes and continued, "I want you both to promise me that you will stay in the backyard today, okay?"

Dick and I nodded yes, finished our toast, and scurried out to the backyard to play. When we got outside, Dick said, "Let's play tag," and he reached out and touched me, "Tag, you're it!"

I laughed and immediately chased Dick. I chased him around

and around until we found ourselves in the front yard near the gypsy families' broken bottles. The gypsy children quickly joined our fun. I tagged one of the other older boys, and he turned to tag Dick. Dick got excited and ran over to tag me, too hard, and I fell to the ground, cutting my leg on one of the broken beer bottles. I started to cry when I saw blood spurting from the gash in my left leg, and I screamed for my mom.

Dick ran to the restaurant yelling, "Mom, Mom. Come quick. Janie's hurt."

Mom dropped her towel, and flew out of the front restaurant door, to find out what had happened to me. A crowd of children surrounded me as she approached. Mom pushed through the people and found me sitting on the ground next to the broken bottles, in a pool of blood.

Upset by what she saw, Mom turned to Dick and yelled, "I thought I told you not to go out in front of the restaurant to play." Then she barked, "What's the matter with you, Dick? You didn't listen to me, did you?"

Then she turned to me: "I should just let you bleed to death, you damn little shit!"

The crowd went silent; the children started to back away. Mom bent over, grabbed my hand, and with one swift jerk lifted me to my feet, grabbed my arm, and walked me fast to the restaurant's front door, through the busy café, and into the kitchen. I cried the whole time, drawing attention from the customers there.

When Woody saw us rushing towards the kitchen, he yelled with fire in his voice and eyes, "Mickey, get that damn bloody kid out of here!"

Mom grabbed a washcloth from the sink and tried to stop the blood shooting from the gash on my leg, but she couldn't stop it. She grabbed a clean towel from the drawer and tied a makeshift tourniquet around my upper leg.

Woody's voice rang out again, "Those damn kids are nothing but a pain in the neck. I can't believe that I let you bring them with us. They should have gone and lived with their father."

Mom looked at Woody with frustration, then grabbed the car keys, hoisted me into the car, and drove me to the hospital. After we were through, I had ten stitches.

Three weeks passed and I hurt myself again. Dick and I were playing outside in the backyard at the tree with the homemade tire swing. The swing was too low to the ground so Dick told me to get a shovel from the shed to dig a hole deeper under the tire.

As I ran to get the shovel, Dick climbed the tree to lift the tire so I could shovel the dirt from beneath it. I started to dig into the hard-packed dirt, stabbing it with the shovel, but I was unable to break the ground.

Then Dick suggested another way: "Janie, put the shovel down next to the dirt. Jump up on the top of the shovel's edge, and try to break up the dirt."

I tried jumping on it a few times; then I put the shovel up above my head and with all my strength drove it hard to the ground. Once . . . twice . . . three times . . . on the fourth attempt I missed the ground and jammed the hard edge of the shovel into my foot. My foot shivered with pain. I screamed, and the tears flowed when I saw the blood streaming from the gash in my right foot.

Dick jumped from the tree limb and ran into the restaurant's back door. He ran through the kitchen and out to Mom, who was waiting tables.

"Mom come quick. Janie cut her foot, and she's bleeding all over!"

Mom put the food down and ran through the back door and out to the swing: "What in the hell are you two doing out here with that shovel? I can't leave you two alone for a few hours without you getting into trouble around here!" She picked me up and carried me to the kitchen sink.

Woody watched her wipe blood from my foot: "What now?"

"Janie cut her foot with a shovel that you put in the shed!"

"What were they doing with that shovel anyway?"

"It's entirely your fault! I told you to lock that shed!"

"I can't believe it. I never wanted those kids to be here in the first place!" Woody yelled.

The customers were watching Woody through the serving window just behind the counter. After he realized everyone was staring at him, he turned and said nicely, "Mickey, take Janie to the hospital. She needs stitches." Looking again towards the concerned customers, he said politely, "Dick can stay with me until you get back." Then he walked over to Mom near the sink and whispered, "Get that bloody brat out of my kitchen now!"

Mom wrapped my foot with a clean towel and drove me to the hospital. I had three stitches and was lucky I didn't break any bones. When we returned home three hours later, Mom carried me to the couch and said firmly, "I don't ever want to see you get hurt again."

Then she grabbed Dick's arm, slapped him on the butt, and yelled, "You are grounded! You disobeyed me today, and your sister got hurt because of it. Now I want you to stay here and take care of her while I go back to work. Is that clear?"

Dick nodded yes, his eyes filled with tears.

When Mom returned to work next door, Dick sat down next to me, tearing up again, and said, "I'm sorry I got you hurt."

I saw his sad eyes, took his hand: "I love you Dick. I'll be okay."

Dick pulled out a book and read to me on the couch, and we soon fell asleep.

The next day Woody made it clear to us that strict discipline and order were going to be our way of life. As a matter of fact, Woody's use of authority became our child labor. He said we had to earn our keep if we wanted to eat—he made us accountable for cleaning the house, and he kept us busy in the kitchen. We had to make the beds every day, and if we missed a specific fold or tuck, Woody pulled it all apart and made us do it all over again until it was right.

Afterwards, Woody brought out a huge sack of potatoes and set it just outside the kitchen door. He had us sit on a wooden box and peel all of the potatoes. When we finished, he had us pick up the shavings and toss them into the big trash burner in the back.

One morning Dick and I were in the restaurant sweeping the floor and wiping the tables. Dick went into the men's rest room and came out with a handful of rubber balloons.

"Hey Janie, come here. Look what I found in the bathroom."

I picked up the balloon. It was slimy, cold, and wet. Dick blew up one of the balloons, and it stretched out long and narrow like the balloons at the fair, though these looked somehow different. We both blew them up and let them go, swirling through the air.

"Come on, Janie. Let's go outside and put some water in them."

Dick held one up to the outdoor water faucet and filled it with water. It stretched to about two feet. He tied the end in a knot, filled another, and handed it to me. I could barely hold onto the thing; it bent in half and wiggled out of my hands.

"Come on, Janie. Let's go out in front and see if we can hit a moving car with them."

We each picked up a full balloon and ran outdoors to the front of the restaurant. We climbed up on the back end of a pickup and waited for a vehicle to come by. We each threw a couple of balloons, missing our targets completely. The cars and semis went too fast for us to hit.

Then Dick said, "Janie, let's throw our balloons together, and see if we can hit one. Get ready."

I held my balloon above my head with both hands, watching as a car approached. Then Dick said, "One, two, three—throw!"

We both tossed our balloons and missed again. We laughed, and Dick said, "Come on. Let's go get some more!"

We ran back to the men's room, grabbed more balloons, filled them with water, and rushed back to our launch pad. This time we decided to stay on the ground closer to the road. Soon a car drove by.

"Get ready," Dick said. I held a balloon up over my head, and when the car got close enough he repeated, "One, two, three—throw!"

We threw the balloons with all our strength. Dick's balloon hit the car's windshield, and mine fell to the ground. The car screeched to a stop and a man got out: "You damn kids. What in the world do you think you're doing? You could have killed us."

Dick and I turned and ran for our lives. Mom had heard the tires screech, and she came outside to see what the man was yelling about.

He shouted, "Some little shits just threw a water-filled condom at me out here, and they ran to the back of your restaurant. If those are your kids, you better tan their hides!"

Mom was outraged. She apologized to the man and came marching after us. We stood behind a tree, hoping she wouldn't see us. But she could see the twenty-or-so balloons on the ground next to the water faucet.

"Dick and Jane, come here right now!"

We stepped out from behind the tree and walked up to her.

"What in the hell are you doing with these rubbers?" She fumed, picking one up. "These are not balloons; these are rubbers! Where did you get these?"

"I found them in a box on the floor near the machine in the men's room," Dick explained.

"These are very expensive. They're not balloons. These are men's rubbers!" She spanked us both on the butt and told us to get in the house and stay there for the rest of the day.

After we did that, Woody and Mom made sure we had even more to do so we would stay out of trouble. They assigned other chores to us every day, and when Woody came home at the end of the day, he made us stand at attention near the kitchen table while he inspected our work.

Mom was so in love with Woody. She was blinded by her love. She didn't notice his extreme demands, his unreasonable expectations of young children. We had to do what he said, no matter what.

From my perspective, Woody had taken charge of us, and we had to carry out his orders or he'd spank us with his leather shaving strap. Mom couldn't control us, and she liked his stern leadership. She loved being his wife; he meant more to her than we did.

Later that same week, the two closed up the restaurant, and we took Woody to the train station. He'd been reinstated in the U.S. Marine Corps, and he had to report to Camp Lejeune, North Carolina, for a week. Mother, Dick, and I were going to visit Grandma MoMo and Grandpa Bill in Jonesboro, Indiana.

4

On a hot sunny morning we dropped Woody off at the Marion Train Station. Mom had the radio blasting, and Dick got to sit in the front passenger seat. He held the map, changed the radio station, and opened a beer for Mom when she wanted one. I got to stretch out in the back.

We saw a lot of cornfields, and every time we drove past a stinking cow pasture we'd hold our noses and say, "Mom put the pedal to the metal." She'd push the gas to the floor, and we held our noses 'til we turned purple. Who could hold their breath the longest? Dick always won.

After an hour on the road, we saw a sign that read: "Jonesboro, population 510." The quaint town was three blocks long, its streets made of brick blocks that sounded like thunder as we drove over them. Jonesboro had a meat market, grocery store, variety store, drug store, and a yarn and needle shop. One whole block was my Grandpa Bill's gas station, auto repair, plus the fire station and an ice-cream parlor.

Mom drove up to Grandpa's gas station and beeped the horn, and Grandpa Bill walked proudly out of the garage in his greasy gray overalls. Dick opened the car door and ran to Grandpa, who flung him up into the air and then rubbed his oily, whiskered face all over Dick's face. I screamed for Grandpa's attention, and he walked over to the car, lifted me right through the window, and kissed me on my cheek.

"It's so good to see you and the kids," he said to Mom. She gave him a hug; then we went straight to the ice-cream parlor for a cone.

My Grandpa Bill Harris was my step-grandfather. He was the smart businessman who had opened up the first retail store in the town in the 1930s. Now he ran a third of the town's businesses. A spunky dark-haired man in his early fifties, he earlier had been a prize-winning body builder, known as "Mr. Atlas."

After we finished our ice-cream cones, Mom told us to get back into the car so we could go up to the house where Grandma MoMo, my mother's mom was waiting. We drove on past the little schoolhouse and straight down the red-bricked street to the rambler at the top of the hill.

The rambler had two bedrooms and a bath with a big picture window in front. It was built on a slope with sidewalks in front and huge apple trees in the backyard. Grandma MoMo grew great big tomatoes and had a few chickens running around the yard.

When we pulled up in front, Grandma MoMo ran to the car and engulfed us with hugs and kisses. Tears ran down Mom's cheeks the minute she saw Grandma MoMo. In her early sixties, she had had her gray hair permed and styled. She wore costume-jewelry earrings and a beaded necklace with her housedress.

"Come on into the house. I made you some chocolate-chip cookies, and I have a nice cold glass of Coke waiting for you in the ice box," she said.

Grandma MoMo's house smelled liked fresh-baked cookies, and everything in the house was tidy. It was such a nice feeling to be treat-

18

ed so special. She was the one I loved more than anyone, and she loved me in return.

As Mom and Grandma talked, Dick and I ran outside to play. That evening after Grandpa got home, we ate Grandma's fried chicken at the dining-room table. Afterwards, we helped her wash the dishes and sweep the floor. Grandma was impressed with our eagerness to help.

Then Grandpa took Dick and me for a walk to the town park, which he had built. We teeter-tottered, slid down the long slide, and swang on the swings he'd built too. That night Dick and I got to sleep on a soft bed made up with fresh-smelling sheets. We could hear our grandparents and mom talking in the living room as we fell asleep. I felt so safe—particularly because Woody wasn't around.

The next day, we all went to church, and afterwards we went to town to celebrate "Bill Harris Day." Grandpa was going to retire, and the people of the town were gathering to honor him for his services. He had been the fire chief for twenty-five years.

We went to the fire station that Grandpa built behind his gas station. It housed the town's fire truck. Dick climbed up on top of the water pumps, and Grandpa put me next to him in the driver's seat and drove the truck to the end of Main Street, where the parade was going to start.

People filled both sides of the street as we drove through, waving our hands as the crowd cheered. After the short parade, we drove to the small park and enjoyed the home-cooked food that everyone shared. That was one of the best days of my life.

We stayed there with our grandparents for eight weeks, and then Mom started to pack up our things. This time Dick wasn't coming with us.

Before we left, Grandma MoMo whispered to me to follow her to the living room. We sat down on the couch, where I could see the photographs of Dick and me on the wall next to her chair. She said I looked sad in that picture, and she gave me a "Jimmy Doll" to keep me company since Dick was staying with them. I loved my Grandma MoMo so much. She knew I was sad, but I couldn't tell her why. I knew Mom and I were going back to live with Woody, and he might kill both of us if I told.

As we drove away, tears ran down my face as I turned around and looked out the back window for a last glimpse of my brother, my best friend, my security. As we drove farther, I began to cry out loud. I was brokenhearted.

Mom said, "I know you miss your brother, but we don't have enough money or room to keep both of you. It's just better this way for now. Dick will have his own room, and he can go to school, and he can help around the house. I know it's hard, but you'll just have to learn to adjust to changes in your life."

I cried myself to sleep. I felt I had lost the only real friend I ever knew. I hated Mom for taking Dick away from me. And now I would have to deal with Woody again—Mom said he would be back at the restaurant. I was afraid. He scared me. But I couldn't tell her about the things he did.

5

When we got back to the restaurant, Woody already had it open for business. Mom was so excited to see him I thought she was going to drive the car right into the kitchen. I stood in the doorway and watched them kiss like young honeymooners. Woody didn't even notice I was there watching them. So I went back outside and got my pillow and blanket to bring into the house.

When I opened the back screen door I could see that nothing had been cleaned or picked up. Dishes were piled in the sink, the bed wasn't made, and newspapers covered the kitchen table. Beer cans were all over the floor and counters, and the place smelled like a tavern. I knew I'd have to clean it up, and now I wouldn't have my brother to help me.

Mom finally came back to the house and helped me pick up the mess. Then she turned on the radio on and went back to the restaurant to work. I sat and listened to a scary show called *The Squeaking Door,* then sang along to the music. That was the only entertainment I ever had while waiting for Mom to come home with dinner.

One evening, Mom stayed at the restaurant until it closed, and Woody came home instead. He brought me some supper, then sat me at the kitchen table, and watched me eat it. When I finished, I went back to the radio, and he sat on the couch next to me. Finally, he leaned over with a smile, picked me up, and said, "Come on, baby doll. I'm going to give you a bath tonight, and you're going to make Daddy very happy."

He carried me into the bedroom, sat me down on the bed, and began to remove my clothes. Then he filled the tub with warm water and lowered me into it. Woody stripped to his underwear and got down on his knees next to the tub. He reached down with a bar of soap and a washcloth and began to wash me. He slowly scrubbed my back, arms, and then my chest. I felt nervous but didn't know why.

Woody washed my feet, then started moving the washcloth up my legs. "We have to wash this too," he said as he washed what I then called my "pee-pee." As Woody rubbed my private parts, he breathed faster and faster. He started to sweat, and he started to bang himself against the tub.

I was four years old by this time, and I hated what he was doing. I knew it wasn't right because my mom never washed me like that. She always had me wash myself "down there," telling me to keep my private parts clean.

When he was done breathing hard, Woody stood up. I could see that he didn't have any pants on, not even underwear. His pee-pee was ugly!

He said then and many times afterwards, "You make Daddy so happy! Now remember: This is our little secret. Don't ever tell anyone about this or I will kill you! Now, get into your pajamas and go lay down on the couch where you belong."

That night when Mom got home, I pretended to be fast asleep. I wanted to tell her what he did, but I was afraid Woody would hear me. I felt so sad. I couldn't run and hide to get away. The only thing I could do was to pretend it didn't happen. Then and later, whenever Woody did that, I ran to the couch to tell my Jimmy Doll what had happened and silently cried myself to sleep.

The next morning Mom and Woody both went back to work, and I had to stay home alone again. I listened to the radio and did my chores alone. A week later, Woody came home alone again. He brought me a plate of dinner, and after I finished eating, he carried me into the bedroom and put me onto the bed. He climbed onto the bed and hovered over me like a huge dark cloud.

I was petrified that he might crush me. I didn't understand this! Dressed only in his shorts, he rocked his body over the top of me, rubbing his private part on my legs and belly. He breathed heavily and grunted and groaned as he increased the rocking. Suddenly, warm pee came out of his thing and poured all over me. In an instant he stopped rocking, took a deep breath, and rolled over on his back beside me, breathing quietly.

I lay still, afraid to move from the warm, soaked bed. He stared at the bedroom ceiling for some time. I didn't understand what had happened. Then Woody rolled to his side and told me how much he loved me, and how I made Daddy feel so happy.

He got up from the bed, filled the tub with warm water, removed my clothes, and put me into the tub. I washed myself this time and put on my pajamas without saying a word. After I went to the couch to curl up under my blanket, he came over to me and whispered into my ear, "Now remember Janie, this is our little secret. You can't tell anyone about this or I'll really hurt you or maybe even kill you and your mom! Do you understand?"

I nodded in fear and tried to bury my thoughts. I didn't want to die. I didn't want to get hurt. I felt trapped, and I put Jimmy Doll on the outside of the couch so he could protect me from Woody.

One night when there was thunder, Mom came home after closing up the restaurant. She was worn out from working so much. She walked right over to Woody, kissed him on the cheek, and said, "I want to thank you for giving Janie her baths. It's been so nice to be able to come home and see her tucked in and sound asleep."

Later that evening, Woody left for the bar across the street. I got up and went to sit on a kitchen chair. The lightning scared me, and I hugged my Jimmy Doll every time the thunder cracked. Without saying a word, I listened to Mom talk about how hard she worked. She complained about her sore back and feet. I wanted to tell her about my scary day with Woody. I wanted to tell her out loud that he was always bothering me and that he hurt me where he touched me.

I watched Mom fill the tub with water. She lit a few candles, poured herself a glass of wine, and stepped in. Then I crawled back onto the couch, put the pillow over my head, and slept.

6

Just before Christmas of 1945, Woody got orders from the U.S. Marines to report to Camp Lejeune, North Carolina, on February 18, 1946. The owner got new renters to run the roadside restaurant, and we packed up our things and headed down the road.

The sun was hot, and all the windows were down as we traveled across the countryside with the radio blasting. Mom looked pretty in her red sundress with her pointed sunglasses and straw hat. Woody outfitted himself in his military boots and a white, tight T-shirt tucked into camouflaged fatigues. I wore shorts and a blouse. Mom put a cooler packed full of sandwiches and beer on the floor next to me in the back seat. She nearly sat on Woody's lap for the first part of the trip. She was happy she didn't have to work at the restaurant any longer. I was happy to get out of that greasy, secluded house.

After twelve hours on the road, we saw a sign reading "Camp Lejeune Marine Base, Straight Ahead." Woody drove up to the gate. He pulled out his billfold and presented his ID and orders. The marine there signaled a guard inside the small station, and the heavy gate rose for us to pass. When the heavy iron arm fell back into position, it clanged like the closing of a jail cell. This would be my life "with the military."

Woody drove down a paved road and past some big brick buildings he called "barracks." Mom beamed at the sight of hundreds of uniformed men marching in the open courtyard. Then Woody pulled into the driveway of a double bungalow and said, "The unit on the left is our new home, and Janie will have her own bedroom!"

Our bodies were stiff from the long ride. After stretching, I rushed to see if there was a lock on my bedroom door. A hallway separated the two *lockless* bedrooms. There was a small bathroom down the hall and a fully supplied kitchen behind a living room, about 12 feet by 12 feet. The military had furnished the house, as well as the packing of our personal things and their delivery the next day.

Every morning at sunrise, I could hear the bugle blowing taps in the courtyard. Mom shuffled into the kitchen to make coffee while Woody showered and shaved. He looked clean in his new crew cut, his shoes shined and uniform freshly pressed. Master Sgt. Woodard Allen was a noncommissioned officer, ranking just below a master gunnery sergeant. What might the marines have said if they knew he was molesting me every chance he got!

Every day after a cup of coffee, Woody headed out the door, and Mom hopped back into bed for a few more hours of sleep before taking me to school.

Later that first day, Mom stood in the kitchen putting some dishes away, when she saw a blond-haired boy playing in the dirt just outside the kitchen window over the sink. She said, "Janie, come here. I want to tell you something."

"Do you see that kid right there playing in the dirt?"

"Yes," I said.

"Janie, I don't ever want to see you playing with that little boy. I don't know what in the world is wrong with his mother." She looked at me sternly and turned back to look out the window. "He's always playing in that dirt, and no one ever changes his dirty diapers."

"Okay, Mom," I said, and went back into the living room to unpack. Each time I returned to the kitchen with stuff, I saw her looking out at that dirty little boy.

Mom unpacked more dishes, several times repeating, "I can't understand why that mother lets him play with those cars and trucks alone in the dirt. His face and whole body is full of dirt. I think someone needs to take care of him properly. He is always filthy dirty, and he stinks. I can see his diapers are hanging from his butt because they are so full of poop. I don't want you ever to play with that 'Filthy McNasty'!"

I nodded to let her know I was listening and kept on doing my chores. I didn't think much about it—I was five years old now, and I didn't want to play with a kid in diapers.

Later that day we went to the commissary, where we picked up groceries, clothes, and pretty much anything we needed. It took us about two weeks to settle into our home.

Almost every night after dinner, Mom put me to bed and then she and Woody went to the bar. They met a whole lot of new friends at the canteen, who nicknamed them "Woody Woodpecker" and "Mickey Mouse."

One night after the two of them came home, the smell of fried bologna woke me. I was hungry and wanted to get up and eat with them but knew Woody would yell at me to get back in bed. I sat up, took deep breaths of toasted bread and fried bologna, then waited for Mom and Woody to go to bed . . .

The next morning at daylight, the house was quiet. My throat was dry, and I was thirsty. I couldn't wait any longer for Mom to wake up, so I tiptoed into the kitchen. I drank a glass of water and opened the refrigerator to see whether there was anything to eat. I saw two cu-

cumbers and didn't think Mom would care if I took one to eat.

I was standing by the kitchen sink chewing on the cucumber when Woody came out of the bedroom. He walked over in his skivvies and grabbed the cucumber from my hand. "What's the matter with you? You can't eat this green cucumber! You're supposed to peel this before you eat it."

Then he grabbed my arms, pulled me toward him, and reached into a kitchen drawer for a roll of gray electrical tape. He ripped off a piece of tape and put it across my mouth. Then he taped my arms behind my back and said, "This will keep your damn mouth quiet, you little bitch! Now, I don't want you to say a word until we get up!"

Woody opened the small closet door, pushed me into it, and said again, "I don't want to hear or see you out here again until I get up. Do you hear?"

I nodded, and he shut the door. I was scared. I had a hard time breathing because the electrical tape sealing my lips together pushed up against the bottom of my nose. It was pitch-dark in the closet, and with arms taped behind my back I was paralyzed. If I pounded on the walls with my feet, Mom might hear it—but I was afraid Woody would come and push my mouth in or break my legs. I shook all over, silently crying. Finally I kneeled and rested my forehead on the floor, my chest over my legs, my arms still behind my back. I was helpless! I didn't dare curl up on my side—I didn't think I could get back on my feet. For a couple of hours I was motionless, legs, arms, and body burning in pain. Then I fell on my side. I wanted to scream for Mom, but if Woody came he wouldn't hesitate to hurt me more. I wanted to bang my head on the wall, but I just shook in fear and waited . . . waited . . .

Finally, Mom opened the door to find me taped up and curled on the floor. She helped me to my feet and with one swift motion peeled the tape from my mouth, pulling the hair from my face. Then she turned me around and pulled the tape from my wrists. As I moved my arms forward, I screamed with pain. She sat me at the kitchen table and rubbed lotion on the red marks on my face and wrists. She knew I'd been tied up for quite awhile. I grabbed her waist and held on to her so hard she had to pry my hands from her back.

"Goddamit, Woody. Why did you put this tape on my daughter?"

"Because she was out of bed before we got up, and I found her eating a green cucumber at the sink!" he yelled from the bathroom.

Mom looked at me and said, "Janie, you've got to learn not to make him mad. See what happened to you because you didn't stay in your bedroom until we got up?"

I looked up at Mom with tears in my eyes. I had thought she would help me get away from Woody. Why didn't she understand how hungry I was? But I could see in her eyes and hear in the tone of her voice that she didn't comprehend how mean Woody was to me and what he'd been doing. I said, "I want to go and live with Grandma MoMo."

"No! You must stay with me because I'm your mother!"

With more tears, I said, "Okay. I won't upset Woody again. I promise."

"Okay, then. Go to you room and get dressed."

From that day on, I never trusted Woody *or* Mom. I never got out of bed before she did, and I was never able to forgive her or him for doing that to me. I still have nightmares thinking about it.

Later that night, Mom and Woody got into a big fight after they came back from the bar. I could hear her swearing at him and saying, "I saw you flirting with that woman at the bar."

"Yeah, and I saw you with that other guy on the dance floor. You were shaking everything that you've got at him!"

I heard Woody pushing the kitchen chair back as he stood and the smack of flesh when he hit Mom across the side of her face. Then there was a thump, followed by a crashing boom as he pushed her hard to the floor.

I jumped up and ran to the kitchen yelling, "Stop it! Stop hitting my Mom!"

"Janie, get back into the bedroom!" Mom yelled from the floor, her lip bleeding.

I ran to Woody and punched him in the leg as hard as I could.

"You little bitch!" He picked up his right leg and kicked me in the stomach, sending me clear across the kitchen into the living area, so that I hit my head on the edge of the couch. "Get back to your room, you little bitch!"

Mom ran to pick me up off the floor. She held the back of my bloody head and started to cry. Woody's rage was out of control. She feared for our lives, and she ran barefoot from the house, carrying me to the house across the street. She pounded on the door, but the house was dark and no one answered.

She turned to see whether Woody was following us. Then she looked to see whether there were lights on in Filthy McNasty's house next door. She ran over and pounded on the door.

We could hear Woody: "I'll kill both of you when I get my hands on you."

Filthy McNasty's mother answered the door, holding a beer in one hand and a cigarette in the other. In her mid-twenties, she had beautiful, big, brown eyes and long, black hair. She was a tall slender woman with a Southern accent.

She looked at us with concern. "What happened to you honey? Please come in, and let me help you."

Tears rolled down Mom's face and I shook like a leaf. Mom looked at Filthy's mother and said, "I'm sorry to bother you, but could you please help us? My husband has been drinking, and he's lost his mind."

Filthy's mom led us into the kitchen. She grabbed a clean towel and pressed it hard against the cut on my head.

"I'm a nurse over at the hospital," she said as she looked at my cut.

"I'm sure you'll be okay, honey." Then she went to the icebox and gave me a piece of ice wrapped in a towel. "Put this on your head, dear. It will help keep the swelling down." Then she gave me a baby aspirin for the pain.

"Thank you," I said.

Filthy's mom looked at my mother and offered, "How about a cold beer and a cigarette to calm you down?"

Minutes later, Filthy McNasty showed up at the kitchen door. His face was clean, and he had on a clean diaper. He stood in the doorway watching us. His eyes were kind. He could see that I was crying.

His mom said, "Come here, honey."

Filthy McNasty bent down, picked up his blanket, and walked over to me. He looked at me, placed his blanket across my legs, and smiled. Somehow that made me feel better.

His mother introduced us: "This is my sweet son, Bobby, and my name is Alice."

"This is my daughter, Janie, and my name is Mickey. We live right next door."

The two moms sat at the kitchen table and talked until Alice's husband, Tom, came home. He was a tall, thin man with piercing blue eyes. Alice told him what had happened, and Tom went to over to our house to talk with Woody.

We waited with Alice and Bobby for another hour or so; then we heard both Tom and Woody coming toward the house. When they entered, Woody walked over to Mom, who was sitting at the kitchen table. He kneeled and put his hands on hers, saying softly, "I love you so much. I'm sorry I lost my temper. I don't know what I was thinking. You are so beautiful, and I don't know what I'd do without you."

Mom fiery green eyes looked into his, and she said, "I will come home this one time. But if you ever hit me again, I will divorce you."

Woody said, "Oh, honey, I love you so much. Please, please forgive me. I promise I'll never hurt you again."

Her eyes softened, and they smiled at each other. "Okay, I love you too! It's that stinking booze. Sometimes it just gets out of hand!"

Everyone shook hands, and the three of us walked home together. Woody kept rubbing Mom's shoulders and saying how much he loved her. She smiled back, willing to forget his fury.

I hated Woody for what he'd done. He never apologized to me, and Mom never gave it another thought as far as I could see! Her threat to leave him never stopped him from coming into my room at night. I lived with that nightmare, the fear that he might come, and sometimes he did.

Mom and I became good friends with Alice and Bobby. Mom helped keep Bobby out of the dirt while Alice was at work. But it wasn't long before Bobby's father received new orders, and they had to pack up their things and move on. I would miss them—I never had any long-term friends while living on a military base. I remember waving goodbye to them—and Bobby gave me his blanket.

On June 6, 1947, Mom received a call from Grandma Etta Mae McCormick saying that Bus McCormick, my birth father, had died of cancer.

We went to Jonesboro, Indiana, to Grandma MoMo's house to pick up Dick, then drove to Logansport, Indiana, where the McCormick family lived. It was the middle of the week, but Dick and I dressed in our best clothes. Woody and Mom dressed in casual summer clothes.

We drove up to a well-kept farmhouse, and my Uncle Jimmy ran to the car. He was handsome, of slim build, about 30 years old. He had a great big smile, and he spoke softly. Approaching the car with arms wide, he said, "So, this must be Dick and Janie. I'm so happy to see you!"

Mom got out of the car and with a slight smile said, "Hi Jimmy. I'm sorry to hear about Bus. I felt I should at least bring the children to say goodbye to their father."

Woody got out of the driver's seat, leaned against the car, and lit a cigarette. He pulled out his flask and took a swallow.

Jimmy thanked Mom with a gentle handshake as he invited them into the house. But Mom and Woody refused his invitation. The McCormick family still worked the farm where my father and his brother, Uncle Jimmy, had grown up. She never liked any of the family's customs and so she asked Jimmy to take Dick and me into the house.

He smiled and said, "I'd be happy to take them." He picked me up like a feather and carried me in one strong arm while Dick tagged along on his right side, almost running to keep up with Jimmy's long strides. "Look at how you two have grown! Dick, you sure are the spitting image of your father. And Janie, you are Indiana's beauty."

As we approached the house we saw a lot of people standing outside on the porch, talking and watching as we walked up the porch stairs.

Uncle Jimmy said, "Hey, look what I've got. These are Bus's two children!"

Everyone stopped talking and greeted us with excitement. The house was filled with the aroma of freshly prepared food. Uncle Jimmy took us to Grandma and Grandpa McCormick. We could feel their love as they introduced us to the rest of our relatives and their friends.

Then Uncle Jimmy took our hands and walked us slowly through the crowd to the flower-filled living room, a coffin at one end. Uncle Jimmy lifted me to see my father; he held me tightly as tears rolled down his face. As we approached the coffin, everyone in the room turned to watch.

Uncle Jimmy put his hand on Dick's shoulder and pulled him close. He said, "This is your father. He was a brave man who won a Medal of Honor at the Battle of the Bulge."

My father's body, dressed in his army uniform, was in the wooden coffin. When I looked down at my brother, I saw him crying as he peeked over the edge. Barely tall enough to see inside the coffin, he had to stand on his tiptoes. Uncle Jimmy said, "I know you don't recognize him because he was very sick for a long time. He was so much fun to be around. He always had a big smile for everyone. I never thought he'd be lying in that coffin, dead at thirty-two. He was a good brother, and he loved you kids with all his heart!"

Afterwards, Uncle Jimmy took us to the kitchen for something to eat. Then he walked over to a baby crib sitting on the back porch. He picked up the baby from the crib and said, "Look. I want you to meet your half-brother, Sam McCormick." Little Sam was a plump six-month-old.

Before we left the house, our grandparents gave each of us a hug and kiss. Then Uncle Jimmy walked us back to the car, where Mom and Woody were waiting. He gave them his address and asked Mom to stay in contact with him. Before we drove off, Uncle Jimmy gave us big hugs and said he loved us. We dropped Dick again in Jonesboro and returned to Camp Lejeune.

In the years that followed, I watched several families move in and out of our military neighborhood, but I never met any new neighbors to play with. Woody continued to molest me whenever he could.

7

One night, I woke up to Woody's drunken, loud mouth in the kitchen. He was bragging to Mom that he'd been promoted to senior advisor, responsible for ninety new enlistments at the El Toro Marine Base in California. His orders gave us less than three weeks to report there—by January 15, 1950.

"Does that mean we can move into a bigger house on the base?" Mom asked, as she pulled a frying pan from beneath the stove drawer.

I could hear Woody opening a can of beer and slamming it down on the kitchen table after taking a swallow: "You're right about that! We'll have a bigger place, and we'll hang out with the brass on the base."

I could smell bacon frying. I was starving, but I didn't want to suffer the consequences of asking for something to eat. Mom turned on the radio, and I could hear their feet dancing to the music. When they finished laughing, Mom asked Woody whether we could pick up Dick on the way to California.

I sat up straight in my bed, then tiptoed to the bedroom door so I could hear them better. Suddenly, they both stopped talking. I peeked through the crack in the door and down the hall to see Woody's face turning mad. Then Woody smiled at Mom, reached out and firmly took hold of her arm, and pulled her onto his lap at the kitchen table. I could see he had her sitting on his lap as he did with me. He was touching her like he touched me when we were alone in the kitchen.

Mom smiled and giggled while he fondled her breasts and caressed her legs, then touched her private part. I didn't like him doing that to me, but she seemed to like it. She closed her eyes and moaned softly while he slowly unbuttoned the front of her dress.

Suddenly, Mom jumped from his lap, grabbed the burning bacon pan, and removed it from the fire. Afterwards, she took a sip of beer and flashed a glimpse of her right breast, then said, "Can we please pick up Dick and take him with us? I miss him so much, and I know he'll be a good boy this time!"

"Oh . . . why not! You sure know how to get your way with me, don't you?" Woody smiled.

I saw her smile back, and then I crawled back into bed. I was so happy to hear that Dick was going to come and live with us again. He'd been living with our grandparents for the past five years. I couldn't wait to see my best friend, my security, my brother.

A week later we put our suitcases into the car and headed to Jonesboro to pick him up. We drove all night and into the next day and arrived in Jonesboro at dinner time. We drove right past Grandpa's auto shop and headed directly to my grandparents' home.

Woody honked the horn when we drove into the tarred driveway. I was so excited to see my still-skinny brother. Dick ran out of the house to greet us. He had grown a lot, and he wore glasses. Grandpa Bill and Grandma MoMo followed, wearing grand smiles on their faces.

I could see that Mom was happy to have us all back together again, and I was happy to be there too! It was so nice. Grandma cooked breakfast for us every morning and made sandwiches for lunch. We ate supper at the dining table each night. On Sunday, we went to church. The best thing was that I didn't have to worry about Woody.

We stayed at the house for two weeks, and then we packed up our suitcases and took off for California. Woody and Mom rotated driving detail for the long trip. It took us four days—thirty driving hours—to get across the country. We rode through thirteen states, traveling about 2,200 miles. At night we checked into a motel and ate dinner. Then Mom and Woody went to the bar next door, leaving Dick and me in the room to play cards.

We arrived on time at El Toro Marine Base. At the front gate, Woody showed the guards his papers, and they gave him directions to our new home. We moved into a double bungalow with three bedrooms, a bath and shower, kitchen, living room, dining room, and front porch.

We moved right in, and the next day our things arrived from Camp Lejeune. I was nine years old and my brother was eleven when we moved to El Toro. As usual, we didn't know where anything was, and we had to start making new friends all over again.

One thing never changed—Woody's military methods. He laid down a strict pace of chores for me to follow. Dick, too, had to abide by Woody's expectations and adapt to a military life. Every morning was a routine. Woody got up at 0400 hours. Mom slithered to the kitchen in her bare feet and silk robe to make him a pot of coffee, while he headed for the bathroom to relieve himself of all the beer he'd drunk the night before. Then, in his boxers, he walked down the hall to the kitchen, sat down in the chair where he'd left his cigarettes the night before, lit a Lucky Strike, took a drag, and started coughing.

After he was done, he slammed his coffee cup on the table and walked back to the bathroom to shower and shave. Afterwards, the house always smelled like his spicy cologne. When he left, Mom crawled back into bed, and we three slept in.

During the next few days, we were introduced to the base's local wives' group. The women gave Mom a map of the base, and she registered both of us for school. Earlier I had attended school on a military base while my brother went to a public school in Jonesboro. Going to school was definitely going to be different for him—he hadn't been a military brat before.

One evening, Mom took Dick and me shopping in the commissary, a food and supply store for the military families. We heard the sounding of taps on the commons. Mom and I stopped to put our right hands over our hearts, facing the flag along with everyone else in the store. Dick kept walking. He didn't know he should face the flag at attention until taps ended.

Dick started to laugh at us. Mom grabbed his arm and told him to stand still and face the flag. After the ceremony was done, Mom was embarrassed that he hadn't known how to salute the flag. The people around us gave her some dirty looks, and she apologized for our ignorance. At home in the kitchen, she made both of us practice making the salute.

"Whenever you hear that horn, you need to stop and face the flag or look in the direction of the common-ground area, and stand with your feet together, shoulders back, and place your right hand over your heart. And you don't move until the horn stops blowing."

At first I thought it was fun. But Mom was so embarrassed that Dick hadn't known what was expected that she made us practice the salute until it became work. She didn't want anyone to think we were stupid or that she was irresponsible about teaching proper behavior on a marine base.

One night, while Mom prepared dinner, she turned on some symphony orchestra music to get us all in a good mood. She was happy to see Dick reading a book in his bedroom and to see me crocheting a blanket in the living room.

And then Woody came home. He opened a beer and sat down at

the kitchen table, yelling, "Those cock-sucking maggots just can't seem to get it right! I have to baby-sit those sons of bitches all day long. I tell them how to log in information and how to keep the records in order, and they still can't put two and two together. They are the saddest bunch of sucking maggots I've ever seen."

When dinner was just about ready, Mom called Dick and me to set the table. I got up and walked to the kitchen.

Woody yelled, "Get your little hog breaths in here right now. You both better jump when your mother calls you."

Dick said, "I'll be there in a minute!"

Woody strode into Dick's room and said, "Don't you ever talk back to me like that. If I ask you to shit, you'll squat and ask me what color. Now get your ass into the kitchen right now before I go and get the strap!"

We both marched into the kitchen and set the table with precision. Afterwards, Mom said, "Now show your daddy how you learned to stand at attention today."

Dick and I stood next to the front of the sink, put our feet together and our arms straight at our sides, facing the flag near the kitchen door. Woody looked surprised and stood up. He walked back and forth in front of us with his arms behind his back, checking out our posture.

Dick turned to look at Mom and started to giggle.

Instantly Woody shouted, "Dick, keep your eyes on the flag, and get that smile off of your face, soldier!"

Then he looked at me and said, "Janie, get your shoulders back and your chest out!"

I pushed my shoulders back and chest out, holding my breath.

"You are proud marines!" he commanded.

We stood at attention, staring at the flag. Then he said "Starting this Saturday at 0500 hours, I will inspect each of your rooms. Your beds, clothes, and toys must pass my inspection before you can go out and play. If I find anything out of place, you will have to remain in your rooms until it's perfect. Is that clear?"

"Yes sir," we said.

"What did you say?" he yelled.

"Yes sir!"

"Okay then, let's sit down and eat!"

We sat down, and Mom said grace. Then Woody started to bark at Dick: "Sit up straight in that chair." He picked up the plate of pork chops, took a couple of pieces, and passed the plate to Dick.

Dick took the plate with his left hand, selected the smallest chop, and passed the plate to Mom. She took the plate in her left hand, served herself a pork chop, and passed the plate to me. I took it with both hands because it was so heavy. I balanced it on the table, stabbed a pork chop, put it on my plate, and passed the plate back to Woody.

This routine repeated itself until all of the food was distributed around the table. We all started to eat at the same time, and soon everyone's plate was empty except mine. Patiently they waited for me to finish eating everything on my plate, but I was jam-packed full.

"If you take food and put it on your plate, you must eat it," Woody said.

"But I'm full, and I can't finish it."

"Okay then, you will sit here until you finish that plate."

Woody got up and went out the kitchen door. Mom didn't say a word. Dick helped clean up the kitchen before going back to his room. I sat there for two more hours, picking at my food.

Finally Mom came in and said, "Jane, next time we eat, don't take such large portions. It's better to take small portions and ask for more." She took the plate, then emptied and washed it. I know she didn't tell Woody she was doing that—he would have made me sit there all night.

The next evening when we sat down to dinner, I was careful not to take too-large portions, but when I had finished, I wanted more.

"Would you please pass me that bowl of food?" I politely pointed to the potatoes.

Mom turned to pick up the bowl of potatoes. She seemed happy to see me asking for more food rather than taking too much the first time.

"What did you say?" Woody looked at me. He told Mom to put the bowl down. "Now, what are you asking for?"

I pointed to the bowl of potatoes and said, "I'd like some more of that."

"And what is that called?" Woody said as he stared into my face.

I froze, looking back at Mom and Dick, both awaiting my answer.

"If you want something more to eat at this table, you must say what the item is before we pass it to you. Do you understand that?"

"Yes sir," I replied.

"The food in that dish is called potatoes! Now repeat after me: 'Mom, can you please pass the potatoes?'"

"Mom, can you please pass the potatoes?" I said.

Mom picked up the potatoes and passed them to me. I reached out with both hands and took the bowl of potatoes. I carefully took a small portion, then handed the dish back to Mom.

"Now, it is your responsibility to remember each food item on this table if you are going to request some more of it. Is that clear?"

"Yes sir." I held back my tears.

That evening when Dick and I were cleaning up the kitchen, Dick tried to help me remember what all of the food was called. He made a game of it, and we laughed about it. But no matter how hard I tried, I always forgot the name of the food when I got to the dinner table. Woody always became angry with me, so I finally just refrained from asking for seconds.

The only thing that kept me going that year was Ronny Roach. He was the first "love of my life"! Ronny's dad had also died when he was five years old, and he had a stepfather as mean as mine. We could talk to each other about our home life. We played tag outside during recess, and he always kissed me when he caught me. As the six months passed, we became boyfriend and girlfriend, and we thought we'd get married someday.

Then one day after school in March 1951, Woody sat Dick and me down on the back steps and told us we were moving again.

That broke my heart. But the worst thing I could do was to cry in front of Woody. I held back my tears and made an effort to look happy. My mind ran rapidly: "I don't want to move again. I can't say anything. I must be proud to be a marine brat. I'll learn to take orders and adjust."

But I couldn't stop thinking about Ronny. I knew I'd never see him again. I had to control my feelings or Woody would get off on another of his tantrums, and I would have to pay a steep price.

I learned to control myself and fake my feelings. I learned to act like he wanted me to act. I learned to smile when he wanted me to, putting on a front like any good actor. In fact, I became proficient.

In Woody's eyes, I smiled and jumped exuberantly at the chance to meet new friends. I willingly packed our things when we moved, and I appeared to enjoy being thrown into a new environment. With change after change after change, I became a confused, controlled, confined, and frustrated girl.

On the night he told us we were moving again, I cried and talked to my doll in bed: "I hate Woody! I hate the marines! I want to stay with Ronny!"

Two weeks quickly passed, and with the usual scurry of the military, we packed to move. Before we drove off, Ronny and his mom visited our house. Ronny gave me a bouquet of flowers, then took my hand and led me to the back of the house. I loved the way he looked into my eyes, gave me a big hug and a kiss, and said, "I love you, Janie. I'm going to miss you!"

I cried and gave him a kiss back.

Shortly after that, we left. I remember looking back at him, waving goodbye for the last time. My heart shattered. I felt I would never have that loving feeling again. Mom yelled at me when I couldn't stop crying. I hated her and Woody for taking me away from my first boyfriend.

After a days drive through the Los Padres National Forest to San Francisco, we reached the navy shipyard, where the *Henry Gibbins* transport ship was docked.

8

On April 11, 1951, the four of us couldn't wait to see the *Henry Gibbins.* We checked through the shipyard gate at one o'clock in the afternoon. Our hearts pumped fast as we chattered with each other. A rush of adrenalin hit when we saw the massive four-story "lady."

A sailor dressed in blues directed us to a loading dock where thousands of military families awaited further instruction. Cheers rang out as everyone watched the ship's crane hoist heavy loads into the cargo bay. After parking the car, we nestled into the group of families waiting at the bottom of the boarding plank. When we reached the top of the plank, Woody handed a sailor his papers as he stepped aboard the ship.

"Sir, Sgt. Maj. Woodard Allen reporting, sir!"

For the first time in my life, I saw Woody having to stand at attention and to salute another sailor dressed in white. I liked it.

"Welcome aboard, Sergeant," the lieutenant said as he looked directly at Woody. He reviewed the orders and said, "It says here that we are to move all necessary dependents and automobiles to the Hawaiian area," handing the papers back. "Please follow the enlisted men to your quarters below." Then he looked at Mom and said, "Mrs. Allen and the children will be escorted by Chief Petty Officer Reinhart."

I was relieved to learn that Woody had to stay below with the other couple thousand military personnel. We followed the officer to the lower deck, where we spent the next nine days of our lives in a two-bunk room with a single porthole, occasionally sharing the canteen and the latrine with hundreds of strangers.

After leaving port, our exhilaration on the deck came to a full stop. As the days passed, Mom went to the ship's deck and spent the day tanning, while I ran to the kitchen to get crackers for my brother, who was terribly seasick.

When we cruised into Hawaii's Pearl Harbor, the cabin became busy again. I wrestled with my brother to look out the tiny porthole from the top bunk of our cabin as the morning sun lit the navy warships anchored in the harbor. The hall buzzed with excitement as families gathered their bags for departure.

Mom rushed to get us dressed, and we joined in the shuffle to the outside top deck, where we could see the crews of several kayaks paddling toward the ship to greet us—three or four young, gorgeous, dark-skinned Hawaiian men and women, dressed in (minimal) bright-colored garments and fresh-flower leis.

As the ship docked, we watched the Hawaiian men point to the sailors and then to the water: "You throw money, ah?"

The sailors eagerly reached into their pockets, pulled out coins, and tossed the silver into the water. The Hawaiian men dove into the aqua water to win a handful of loose change. Their welcome felt warm and humbling.

We watched the sailors dock the huge ship and move the metal plank to the top deck. The military men formed a single line for departure, and we pushed our way through the families to the front. For a moment, I looked up and was mesmerized by the array of colors in the water. For a moment I forgot Woody would join us soon.

The ship's horn blasted, and the man on the loud speaker said, "Welcome to Hawaii. We will be unloading family members first. It is 9 A.M., and all of you will be escorted to a check-in area where you and your husbands will come together. Have a great stay in Hawaii."

On the dock below, several Hawaiian men pounded drums in greeting while women motioned smooth, symbolic words with hands and swaying hips. A young man and woman stood at the end of the ship's exit ramp, where the woman placed a hand-made lei around each of our necks and a gentle kiss on each one's cheek. When I looked into the young woman's eyes and felt the warm sun shining on my face, a peaceful feeling filled me.

A sailor dressed in whites gathered all of the families and escorted us to a check-in point, where our passports were checked and stamped. Then we waited. It seemed like a decade before all of the marines were off the ship. When Mom saw Woody walking towards us, she ran to him, making a grand show of her love; everyone watched them kiss and embrace.

Dick looked back at me, rolled his eyes, and said, "Looks like the master sergeant is back!"

The two walked over to us, Woody ordered us to bring the luggage and follow them. We dragged the small handbags and followed the two of them to parking lot, where we stood and watched the hoist unload. Suddenly a loud clang from the ship above attracted everyone's attention: The crane was lowering an armored tank.

While everyone looked at the crane, Woody turned to look at me standing next to him. He looked directly into my eyes, then took a step back and stared at my ten-year-old breasts.

"Come here, my sweet little doll baby. Give your daddy a hug!"

I didn't move. I cringed at the thought of him touching me. I could feel his eyes looking right through my pink cotton dress and panties.

Then Mom said, "Janie, get over there and hug your daddy! He misses you!"

I hesitated but stepped forward. He put his hand behind my back and pulled me close to the front of him where my head came above his belt buckle.

"Didn't you miss your daddy?" He held me so tightly I could feel his thing on my torso. "I sure missed you!"

He whispered. "You and I are going to have a lot of fun here. I can promise you that, my little girl!" Then he looked around to make sure no one saw him caressing my back and behind. In his best brass voice, he barked, "Now, everyone follow me" and led us to the car, which had been parked behind closed gates.

We drove up the west coast on Highway 93, headed for Makaha. It was 80 degrees F., and a soft breeze blew from the Pacific. The mountain was lush green, loaded with gaudy blossoms and tall palms.

Mom navigated and read out information about Oahu. She turned on the radio, to find that all the programs broadcast from Honolulu were in the Hawaiian language. The two English-speaking stations were broadcast from the U.S. Marine station in Kaneohe Bay.

After a forty-minute drive, Woody pulled into the small town of Makaha, and said, "We are going to live near the city of Makaha, in front of Mount Kaala, the highest mountain on Oahu."

He continued driving along the shoreline for another ten or twelve minutes; then he pulled into the driveway of our new home and said, "I've rented a Quonset hut, which faces east and is directly across the street from the highest-breaking waves in Hawaii."

Mom asked, "How did you keep this a secret?"

"I made the arrangements before leaving El Toro. The half-acre, single-family home is four blocks from the local school, twelve miles from the naval base, and just half a block from the ocean."

"Oh my God, honey, you've really outdone yourself." Mom kissed him on the cheek.

Woody drove south another half-mile to show us the U.S. military base and the private beach club for the military personnel and their families. Then he turned around and drove back, pointing left to the road leading to Waianae Elementary School.

Woody drove back to the Quonset hut, which looked like a giant soup can cut lengthwise. There were ridges on its exterior, and its floor was stacked up on stilts to protect it from tidal waves. It had a front and back porch with steps leading up to it, and windows all around. From the front entry we walked into a living room with a brown-carpeted floor and white-curtained windows. The living room led to a long hallway with one large bedroom on the right and two smaller bedrooms to the left. A bathroom and a kitchen were at the end of the hall. The house opened in the back to flat, open grass, where we could play. The base of the mountain was just two blocks away.

The doorbell rang, and the marines delivered our new rattan furniture, beds, and kitchen set, along with all our other packed belongings. Mom sent Woody for hamburgers while we unpacked the boxes and put everything neatly in place. When Woody returned three hours later, it was all set. We ate the burgers, and Woody and Mom decided to go the military beach canteen, about ten minutes away, for cocktails.

Before they left, Mom said, "The sun is going down now, and I want you two children to stay in the house when we are gone. There are wild boars, venomous snakes, and bugs large enough to eat you alive!" Woody and Mom drove away just as the sun set behind the face of the mountain. The yard became pitch black.

We turned on a light at the kitchen table and played gin rummy. After a couple of games, Dick said, "I'm so tired of sitting around and playing cards. I can't wait to go outside and run around."

"Hey, let's play hide-and-seek! Tag, you're it!" I ran down the hall while Dick counted to ten to look for a hiding spot.

"Ready or not, here I come," Dick said.

I was hiding beneath my bed. I could hear the floor creak as Dick walked down the hall towards the living room. Then he tiptoed back to my room. I could see the bottom of his feet as he approached the bed. He stopped right next to my face, and then he jumped on top of the bed, laughed, and said, "I found you. You're it. Start counting!"

I counted to ten, crawled from beneath the bed, and started to look for Dick in our parents' bedroom, where there was a small splash of light coming from the neighbor's front porch. I looked behind the chair, then saw Dick curled up behind Woody's metal trunk. I tiptoed up to him and yelled, "Tag. You're it!"

Dick jumped up with surprise. He climbed off the trunk, jumped to the bed, and yelled, "I hate that goddam Woody." He laughed and continued to jump back and forth from the trunk to the bed saying, "I hate that son-of-a-bitch. He's a sucking bastard."

I jumped up on the bed and mimicked all the swear words as we kept on jumping.

"They always have us clean up after them, those assholes," Dick yelled.

"Yeah, and we always have to stand at attention when Mr. Asshole comes in the door," I yelled.

Suddenly, we heard a scratching sound coming from outside the Quonset hut. Dick stopped jumping and said, "What was that?" He looked at me with big eyes, then looked around the room, while I continued to jump on the bed, screaming nasty language.

Less than a minute passed; then Dick and I joined in running around the house, repeating the crude sentences that Woody said to us every day he was with us.

Then we both heard a louder scratch against the outside of the metal hut. "What was that?" said Dick as we stopped short.

"I don't know!" I whispered.

We heard another scratch against the outside metal.

"I think something is out there." Dick looked frightened.

Then I whispered in his ear, "Let's hide under my bed."

Dick and I ran to my bedroom and crawled beneath the bed. In the dark we heard a scratching just outside the window. We were so scared!

Then we heard the snap of the front-door lock. The door creaked as it opened. Heavy footsteps sounded across the living room and started down the hall towards the kitchen. All of a sudden we each felt a hand grabbing the back of our shirts, and Woody yelled, "You goddam little shits, you better do something about your language. In here, Mickey!"

He dragged us out and up to our feet. "You better wash these kids' mouths out with soap!" He looked at us. "I never want to hear you swear like that again, you little shits!"

Mom ran to the bathroom and came back with a bar of soap. She rubbed the bar against our teeth, then put the soap into our mouths: "I don't ever want to hear you swear again, goddam it! What got into you kids? Have you lost your minds, talking like that?"

We choked and gagged as we spit up the foamy soap.

"Now get to bed," Woody yelled as he pushed us into our separate bedrooms.

I grabbed a clean shirt from the closet, wiped out the inside of my mouth, and eventually cried myself to sleep.

The next day, Mom drove Woody to the military base, and then we shopped at the local stores. That afternoon she drove us to the Waianae Elementary and Intermediate School, where she registered me for fifth grade. The Hawaiian principal gave us a tour of our new school. Its stucco-covered building was in the center of Waianae. The classrooms were small, and all of the children were from the islands. We were scheduled to start the following week—September 21, 1951.

At about 4 P.M., Mom drove us back to the house, then went to pick up Woody at the base. After she drove away, Dick said, "Janie, let's go down by the beach!"

We scurried through our grassy front yard, across the tar road, and out across the sandy beach to put our feet in the roaring ocean. We hadn't been there for more than ten minutes when five Hawaiian boys approached us.

"You *haoles,* go home. We no like you here!" They waved their arms and yelled with clinched fists. "We no like you here. You go back mainland!"

Dick and I were scared—stunned speechless by their strong reaction to us.

"This our island," the locals yelled, "You go back mainland."

Dick and I didn't know what to think. Neither of us had ever been confronted with anything like it. We tried to keep our distance by backing away from them and towards the house as they threatened us face to face.

Finally, the biggest boy rushed up to Dick and pushed him backward. "We no like *haoles.* You go back mainland!"

Another boy pushed me down onto the tar road, skinning my knees. Dick pushed the kid back and shouted, "You better leave my sister alone, you bully!"

Then the biggest boy pushed Dick to the ground. He stayed down, hoping they'd leave us alone. Then one of the younger boys saw my bleeding knees, got scared, and ran away. The other boys followed him, and we ran back to the house and locked the doors. I cried as Dick helped me clean my stone-embedded knees and wash the black tar from our clothes. Now we were afraid of being beaten up at school— we were the only white kids there.

When Mom returned, we told her what had happened. She said, "Oh, you better just stay in your own yard for a couple of days. They'll get used to you two soon enough. Now go get ready for dinner, before your father finds out what kind of trouble you got into!"

The next Monday, the day we were to start school, we were nervous about meeting the kids on the island. Mom drove us to Waianae early that morning so we could meet the principal, who was going to introduce us to our new teacher and classmates.

My brother said to me, "Be brave. We are marines," before he was led to his classroom.

The principal escorted me to my fifth-grade classroom. When he opened the door, everyone in the room turned to stare at me. The principal said, "Good morning. This is Jane, your new *malahini* [newcomer to the islands]." Then he looked at me and said, "Jane, this is Mr. Nakanishi, your *kahuna* [professional skills—in this case, my teacher]."

Mr. Nakanishi said, "I want everyone to say aloha to Jane."

"Aloha, Jane," the class of about twenty locals responded.

"This is your seat, behind Lana," Mr. Nakanishi said.

Lana was a full-blooded Hawaiian. She smiled with her eyes, in a gentle way, showing friendship.

Mom picked us up at 2 P.M., the end of the school day. The car was full of groceries, and her skin was pink from the day's sun. Her long, brunette hair was pulled back into a bun. "How did your day go?" she asked us both.

Dick curled up his nose: "It was fine, but they sure talk funny."

"Yeah, I noticed that too, son, when I was at the store," she said with a sneer.

"Yeah, but at least I was able to understand them. I thought everyone was really nice, and I met Lana [*lah nah*, meaning calm as still waters]. She lives next door to us!"

"Well, here you two were all worked up about those boys pushing you around, and it seems like everything worked out after all!" Mom said.

"I met Alohi, [*ah low hee*, meaning brilliant] in my class, and he lives next door, too," Dick said.

"That's good, son. Maybe both of you will have new friends to play with," Mom smiled with relief. "I have to tell you, the Hawaiians definitely have different ways of doing things from Americans. I read that they have only twelve letters in their alphabet. The vowels are A, E, I, O and U, like ours, but the only consonants they use are H, K, L, M, N, P, and W. And they have a whole different meaning."

Dick and I were confused; we shrugged our shoulders and started to laugh.

"You'll just have to be patient! This is the only school for you to attend. You'll just have to grin and bear it all until you understand the language. You'll get used to it, I promise," Mom said.

9

A week later Dick and I started riding our bikes to school, hoping we wouldn't pass anywhere near the Hawaiian bullies. We stayed away from the beach in front of our place, and for the first few weeks after school we went with Mom to the private military beach, where we could safely swim with other American families.

Each day Mom packed a basket of food, and Dick and I ran to put on our swimsuits. After Mom parked the car in the beach parking lot, we played in the ocean while she tanned next to the stone wall dividing the beach from the lounge. It didn't take long for her to become acquainted with several other American wives—or to flirt with the single military men.

One day, a lot of sailors were at the beach playing volleyball close to where Mom was tanning. Dick and I were fascinated with the seashells washed on shore, and when we found something unusual (at least to us), we'd yell, "Hey, Mom . . . hey, Mom . . . look what we found!"

Dick and I jumped up and down in the water, vying for her attention. She lifted her head to look, then put her head back down and simply ignored us. We went back into the water to look for more. We repeated the scenario several times, finally wrapping the shells in a wet towel and running to her side. Some of the water from the towel dripped on her oiled back. She raised her head, gave us a dirty look, put her head down, and ignored us again.

We persisted, both of us picking up shells: "Look Mom. Look what we found!"

She lifted her head and snarled, "Wait just a minute! Can't you see that I'm trying to relax? Now put those shells down, and go play in the water!"

"Ah . . . come on, Mom. Please come down and play with us?" Dick pleaded.

Mom rolled over, sat up, looked at us, and said, "Okay, go on! I'll be there in a minute!"

Ten minutes passed, and she didn't come down to the beach. Dick and I yelled, "Hey Mom, come on. Come in the water with us. It's great!"

Mom appeared to be cleaning her painted nails. We yelled again and again, and finally she stood up and marched down to the shoreline into the waves breaking at her knees: "Come here, right now!"

Each of us grabbed a shell and ran to her. Mom grabbed the shells from our hands and threw them in the water. "Dammit, I don't want you kids ever to call me 'Mom' when we're at this beach! As a matter of fact, I don't want you to call me "Mom" when we're in public again! I hate it when all of these kids are yelling 'Mom.' All day long, all I hear is some kid yelling 'Mom . . . Mom . . . Mom!'"

She looked at the sailors playing volleyball and sneered, "I don't even look old enough to have children your age! Now get back in the water and leave me alone!"

I started to cry. Dick looked surprised.

She continued, "From now on, if either one of you wants my attention, I expect you to calmly walk up to me and address me as 'Mickey!' Is that clear, Dick and Jane?"

Neither of us said a word.

"Is that clear?

"Yes ma'am," we answered.

"I don't ever want either one of you to call me 'Mom' again when we are here!"

"Okay, Mom," Dick said softly.

Mom squinted. "Good! Now it's getting late, so I want you to pick up your things and get ready to go. Don't forget to rinse yourselves off at the shower near the building."

We left our shells behind, and after that, when we were around other people, we always called our mother "Mickey."

Going to Waianae Elementary was different from school in America. The Territory of Hawaii didn't require that children stand at attention and pledge allegiance to the flag every morning. I had to learn the whole Hawaiian educational system and language along with the other foreigners—the Portuguese, Chinese, Filipino, and Japanese children. I had a slight advantage, however, as everyone on the island had to learn English—the "universal language" of the school. Most of the kids at school liked practicing their speech with Dick and me. But when at the end of the day when school was out, the Hawaiians spoke their own slang, and the foreign kids spoke their native languages too. We learned it all, and soon it became part of our everyday vocabulary.

The Hawaiian teachers were humble, gracious, and soft-spoken. They taught with the "aloha spirit"—the coordination of mind and heart within each person, bringing each person to the self. According to the Hawaiian culture, each person must think and express good feelings to others. The teachers taught each lesson carefully, gently nurturing each child towards harmonious living.

We were taught to love and care for the land and to protect the islands. We soon learned that kindness was to be expressed with tenderness, unity with harmony, humility with modesty, and patience with perseverance.

The Hawaiians worshipped nature. They saw its forces manifested in many forms, to which they ascribed godlike powers. They lived out this philosophy in their daily lives. We learned that Hawaiian gods could be anything, animate or inanimate.

When school let out for the summer, Dick and I decided to go across the street and down a block to the beach in front of our Quonset hut to play. When we got to the beach, we could see the younger kids bodysurfing on waves carrying them to shore. The teenagers were on surfboards in deeper water. We could see that the waves were larger and twice as fierce as the waves on the army reservation.

We watched the teen surfers: when a high wave approached, they lay on their boards, madly paddling with both arms to catch the wave's forward motion. Then in one swift move, they jumped up on their boards, balancing themselves for the ride at the top of the four-story wave.

Those less skilled were thrown into the wave's undercurrent. The wave slapped the surfboard high into the air, and the current sucked the surfers into itself, then turned them around like a washing machine. Sand washed into every pore.

Dick and I ran out to meet the receding waves, then turned and ran back to the shore, laughing as the breaking wave caught up with our backsides.

Lana, my ten-year-old classmate, who lived next door, came over to me and said, "Aloha, you like play ocean, *ae* [yes]?" She had thirteen brothers and sisters, from one to fifteen years of age.

I smiled and said, "Yes, I like to play in the water."

"You no turn back on wave, ae," Lana said seriously.

"Yeah, I see. These waves are huge!" I said as I stared at the ocean.

"You like learn body surf, ae?"

"Yes, that would be fun. How do you do that without drowning?"

"First, you must respect *moana* [the ocean]. You never turn back on *kai* [the sea]," Lana explained.

"Okay. You show me," I replied.

"When you see wave coming, you swim real fast toward wave, and you dive through wave, and you turn around real quick and ride wave all way to beach."

I followed Lana out, and we caught a big wave. We both dove into the wave, and we quickly caught the backside of it. The wave lifted me so high that I could see our Quonset hut a block away. I had never done anything so exciting.

We laughed together and played with the waves for hours. At the end of the day Lana reminded me to show respect for the sea at all times. She looked at me and said, "The ocean is the most powerful and dangerous thing in the world, and you must never turn your back on it. One must always walk out of the ocean facing the sea."

"Okay, Lana. I will always respect the ocean."

"Remember, if you catch a wave the wrong way, it will hold you down and turn you around over and over. You've got to hold your breath for a long time, and you've got to get all the way underneath it, and let the wave go over the top of you. If you don't do that, the wave will turn you over and over, and it will beat you down into the sand." Lana rolled her arms as she talked.

The next day I hurried to the beach to play with Lana. We rode the waves, and then Lana saw a big turtle. She jumped into the water with both hands and grabbed each side of the turtle's shell. The big turtle pulled her through the water, and then she let go and stood up.

"Jane, hold onto my feet after I grab the turtle." Lana dove back into the water and grabbed the turtle's shell again.

I chased after her and dove into the water to grab her feet. The turtle gave us a fast ride. Then we came up for air and did it all over again. We had so much fun, and I was happy to have a girlfriend.

Afterwards, Lana pointed to her big house and said, "You eat my *hale* [house], ae?"

"Okay," I said, following her home.

It was an older, two-story house built on bamboo stilts. I followed Lana in the front door, through the living room, dining room, and into the large kitchen. Her pregnant mother was standing at the counter, mixing up a bowl of fruit for lunch. Her long, wavy, black hair flowed to the middle of her back, in contrast to her bright yellow-flowered *muumuu* (loose dress). A three-year-old boy and two-year-old girl were sitting at the kitchen table, eating fruit. A toddler babbled in his high chair at the end of the table. A fat, shorthaired tabby cat lay on top of the refrigerator, sleeping, and a shepherd dog sat next to the Lana's mother's side, waiting for any morsel she might toss him. A chicken ran around on the back porch, and another pecked crumbs from the kitchen floor.

"Mom, this is Jane, the haole who lives next door, and this is my mom, Pua [flower]," Lana said.

Pua turned to me and with a warm smile said, "Aloha, Jane. You like eat, ae?"

"Yes ma'am," I smiled.

"Please sit. Eat!" Pua pointed to the table, which had five empty chairs.

Lana smiled and patted her Mom's round belly, "Mom is *nui* [big] with *keiki* [a child]. She always with keiki!"

Lana walked over to the table, motioning for me to sit next to her. Pua put a bowl of fruit on the table, and we filled our plates. We listened to Pua hum "My Little Grass Shack" as we quietly ate lunch. Afterwards, Lana picked up our plates, washed them, and put them back down on the table for her other brothers and sisters to use. I was amazed at the harmony of this household.

"Thank you for lunch, ma'am," I said.

Lana took me for a walk through her backyard, where her family raised pigs, cows, horses, vegetables, and fruit. She explained, "*Aina* means that the land is the source of our food. It is our land that gives us our life. We who live in the islands walk upon its earth, breathe its air, drink its water, and eat the food it provides. Hawaii is within us; it is a part of us. If we defile Hawaii, we defile ourselves.

"You are so lucky, Lana," I said.

"Ae, lots of us, we work together. We love and support each other," Lana smiled. "We go play ocean, ae?"

Later that night I thought about how nice it was to have a best friend with a family so different from my own.

10

As the week went on, Mom continued to go alone to the private beach, and she established some close friendships with three American military wives. They chummed around regularly during the day, and at night Woody and Mom often joined them for card games at one of their houses.

One Saturday afternoon, the three couples were going to meet at our house. Mom went into a tizzy preparing food and setting up tables and chairs borrowed from military beach canteen. At 1400 hours, the three couples arrived. One of the couples brought a son, Wally, a seven-year-old with bright red hair and a lot of freckles. Right away we knew Wally wasn't just an ordinary kid—he ran around our house like a wild monkey. Mom told Dick and me to get him out of the house, to take Wally to the beach.

At the beach, Dick and I joined with the islanders who were body-surfing the waves. Wally stopped at the shoreline and watched us. I'd become accustomed to riding the waves, but I knew Wally didn't understand the force that washed at his feet. At first he chased the rushing waves, retreating quickly to the shore to avoid contact with the water. But each time he chased the retreating water, he went a step farther, and the ocean pushed more and more water to the back of his ankles, to his legs, and finally to his total backside.

I watched him closely because I knew that the three-story waves could kill him. I rode the wave in and started towards him before the next wave approached. He was already running after the next swell, which was huge.

Wally chased the receding wave and stopped to watch it build. Before he knew it, the enormous wave crashed down and threw him into the sand, rolling him over and over on the bottom. I was glad to see him alive when he washed up on shore. By then a lot of the kids had gathered to watch him stand up, covered with sand. Everyone laughed—he had sand in every part of his body.

Wally stood on the beach, trying to dig the sand out of his ears, belly button, and the crack of his butt. Finally he pulled down his swimsuit and let his penis dangle free, while he tried to wipe away the sand.

One of the older girls yelled, "Yuck, put that thing back in your pants."

Wally, however, thought it was funny and began to run around the beach after us, waving his penis.

Finally Dick yelled, "Gross. Put that short little pecker away, Wally! Yuck!"

But Wally laughed and continued to tease anyone who came near him. When, finally, he walked up to me, I grabbed the waistband of his swimsuit, pulled it up to his waist, and said, "Wally, this is not funny! It's not right to run around like that. Now stop it, or I'm going to take you back to the house, and tell your mom!"

He knew I was serious, and in the next breath all was forgotten. Dick and I decided to play closer to the shore, with Wally.

When the sun set behind the mountain, I took Wally to our back-yard where we rinsed off the ocean salt. The radio was blasting out music, and the house was filled with smoke as the grown-ups played cards in the kitchen. We helped ourselves to a plate of food on the card table in the living room. Then Dick took Wally into his room to sleep, and I went to bed.

It was about 0200 hours that Sunday morning when everyone went home. Mom stumbled to the bedroom and passed out. Woody turned off the lights and crawled on the floor into my bedroom. He crawled on top of me in my bed and put one hand across my mouth, the other between my legs.

I was pinned down and scared. I couldn't move. All I could do was lie there while he jacked off against my body. I couldn't fight his strength and his breath reeked of booze. I stared at my baby doll in the corner and tried to think about the wonderful day I had at the beach, hoping he would hurry up and get it over with.

After he finished, he grabbed my neck and threatened to kill me if I told anyone. Then he walked out to the bathroom, cleaned himself up, and went to bed.

I cried myself to sleep. I hated him, and I didn't know what to do about it. I wished I were big enough to put him in jail for the rest of his life. He was a sick man; and no treatment would change him. Men like him should never be free to touch a child.

The next day Lana didn't see me at the beach, so she walked to my house and knocked on the front door. Woody answered the door and told Lana to wait outside.

A few minutes later I came to the door. She said, "You come play ocean, ae?"

I didn't smile as usual. I just looked down at the porch floor and said, "Yes. But I have to help Mom clean the house before I can come out and play."

"What's matter, Jane? Lana asked.

"I'll tell you later, Lana. I'll meet you soon, down at the beach. Now you go!" I hurried back into the house, and Lana walked away.

Two hours passed before I joined her. The waves were unusually high, and there was a red flag waving and a sign: "High Surf—Dangerous Shore Break." Lana ran from the water to meet me.

"What's that sign doing there?" I asked

"Oh, high surf means powerful waves started by storms at sea— sometimes thousands of miles away. They make a wave fifty feet high. They're not safe. The waves can hurt anybody, even those who surf a lot. They hurt many surfers' necks and backs," Lana explained.

"They should have posted that sign yesterday, when Wally was here," I said.

"Yeah, that kid is lucky to be alive. The sea knocked him down and almost drowned him. It could have pulled him out to sea and sharks could have got him," Lana said.

"I see what you mean!"

"Now you okay, Jane? Why you sad?"

"Yeah, I'll be okay. I always am!" I smiled.

"What wrong, Jane? You looked scared and upset this morning."

"Me can't tell you, Lana!" I said, then started to cry.

"Why you so sad? Someone hurt you?"

I cried harder. "Me can't tell you, Lana!"

She looked confused. "Me hurt your feelings?"

"No!" I couldn't stop sobbing.

Lana put her arm around me: "You come my house. We talk!"

We ran back to my house first, where I found a note on the refrigerator: "Dick and Jane, we are going out to eat with some friends tonight. Eat the leftovers in the icebox. Love, Mom and Dad."

It was mid-afternoon when we got to Lana's house. We watched her father dig a pit for a *luau* (Hawaiian feast), and then all of her brothers and sisters and I watched Lana's father and three other men chase one of the bigger pigs in the backyard. We laughed as the smart pig squealed and dodged the muddy assailants. After several failures, the four men decided to corner the pig. One of the men pounced on top of the hog, forcing it to the ground. Another helped hold it down, while the other two men rushed to tie its back feet together. They hoisted it into the air by its back feet and secured it to an iron spit. The poor pig squirmed and screamed like a child as Lana's brother instantly shoved a knife into the main artery in its throat. Blood spurted out, and the pig died instantly. Then the men put a big tub beneath the pig to catch the blood.

The pig hung there for a few hours while we played in the backyard. Then the men lowered the dead pig to the ground and cut its stomach open, scooping out the pig's guts with their bare hands. Lana's older brothers buried the guts far from the house. The four men finished digging a deep hole in the ground.

A hot burning fire cradled a kettle of boiling-hot rocks. The men emptied out the boiling water and put the rocks on the ground next to the pit, each occasionally dipping his hands into an icy bucket of water as they filled and lined the pit with alternating layers of hot rocks and banana leaves. After stuffing the pig, the men covered the whole thing with banana leaves and buried it in the pit.

After the pig was buried we ate dinner, and Lana asked me to come up to her bedroom where it was quiet. Lana shared a bedroom with three other sisters. It was crowded and somewhat messy.

We sat down on her bed, and she asked, "What wrong with you, Jane? You can tell me! We best friends!"

I looked at her sadly and said, "It's my stepfather, Lana. He touches me wrong all the time!"

"What you mean?" Lana asked.

Tears rolled down my cheeks. "Last night after everyone left, Woody crawled into my bedroom on his hands and knees. He covered my mouth and he rubbed my privates, between my legs. Most of the time it doesn't hurt me, but last night it did!"

"Jane, that wrong," Lana said.

"He told me that's how fathers love their little girls!"

"No! No, Jane, that wrong! My father never do that nasty thing to me! He not respect you!"

"Promise not to tell anyone I told you this!"

"But Jane, that wrong. He hurts you!"

"No, Lana, you don't understand! Woody will slice my throat open like that pig, and he will kill my mom and brother if he knows I told you!" I looked around the room to see if anyone had heard what I said.

"Jane, you must tell someone. He's a bad man!" Lana pleaded.

"No. Promise me not to tell anyone, Lana. If Woody finds out, he may hurt you too." I grabbed her arms and looked into her face. "You have to promise me you won't tell anyone!"

"Okay, Jane, I promise."

"I better go home now before it gets too dark."

Lana walked me halfway home. She gave me a hug, and we waved goodbye.

When I got home, I felt relieved that someone knew my secret. I crawled into bed, thinking that things would never change with Woody. I didn't know how to stop it. I wanted to slice his throat and hang him to bleed.

Then I heard my brother come in the back door. Dick heard me crying, looked into my room, and asked whether I was okay. I told him I was fine and rolled over and went to sleep.

11

Our whole family was invited to the luau the next evening at
Lana's. A crowd of friends and family members filled her backyard, lit with several torches. And there were tables loaded with fresh
fruit and flowers.

Lana grabbed my arm and led me upstairs. She said, "Did you say
you wanted to get away from that scary stepfather or yours?"

"I would love to get away from him touching me—forever—but
I'm afraid to do it by myself!"

"I am so mad at my mom! I'll go with you!" Lana told me.

"Oh, that would make me so happy!" I grabbed her and put my
arms around her and squeezed tight.

"Okay . . . okay . . . let's go," Lana said as I jumped up and down.

We talked about how we'd run away the next day. It was almost
the end of the summer—September 1, 1953, was to be the first day of
school. We would take off up the mountain—no one would ever look
for us there. After we ate, I went home, lay across my bed, and looked

at the ceiling. I was happy that I would never have to look at that sick Woody again. I just knew no one would ever find us. I went to sleep early, and he didn't come into my room that night. Most of the time he did.

The next morning I got up, took a shower, got dressed, and ran out the door. I saw Lana standing on the side of the road, waving to me. We hugged, then started to walk as we had every school day, towards the school. But when we came to the street where we were supposed to turn, we kept going towards the mountain. Then we ran up the street, laughing and singing. We were happy. She was happy for me, and when I suggested she go home later that day, as if she had been to school, she said, "No! I'm going to stay with friend."

"Then I'm going back! I don't want to get you into trouble because of me running away from Woody."

Lana grabbed my arm. "I your friend! We stick together!"

"Okay! I will always remember that you helped me get away from my stepfather. Thank you from the bottom of my heart," I said with tears in my eyes.

We kept walking up the narrow road until we neared the top of the mountain, where we saw an old shack. Lana ran up to it and knocked on the door. I was afraid that someone would be there and take us back, but no one answered. When we looked in all the windows, we saw that no one lived there and crawled through an open window. We looked in the kitchen for something to eat—by this time we were hungry for lunch. There was nothing to eat so we just laughed and talked. Then it turned serious, as I told her more about my stepfather, weeping again. Lana held me and cried with me. I wept for at least an hour—I had never been able to talk to anyone about what Woody had been doing to me as long as I could remember.

"It started when I was three years old . . . And as I get older, it gets worse and worse. My mom doesn't know anything is going on."

"Jane, how did that ever happen, right in front of your mom?"

"Oh, he waits until she is asleep or passed out, and my brother is a sound sleeper, and Woody just puts his hands on me and jerks off beside my bed."

Lana started to scream, "Oh my god, Jane. How do you get through that?"

"I close my eyes and pretend I like it and then he gets done faster. Then he leaves me alone and goes to his bedroom with my mom. Sometimes I throw up, and I cry myself to sleep all the time."

"I will never forget it as long as I live," Lana said. "I'm sorry you had to live like that, you poor girl. You no go back ever, okay?"

"Okay. I don't ever want to see him again. I will miss my brother, and I love my mom, but she never helped me. I don't think she knows what's been happening. Mom would hate him if she knew."

We stayed in that shack until dark. We found some cigarettes and matches, and we smoked and got dizzy and laughed. We thought we could go back down to the beach and find some clams or snails or something else to eat. When we finally got down to walk on the coral, Lana handed me a snail.

"No way can I eat that raw."

Lana popped it into her mouth, then spit it out.

We continued walking along the shore, close to the water so no one could see us. The moon was bright so we could see pretty well. We went by the Army Reserve beach and we saw people standing at the bar, listening to music. We got down on our hands and knees and crawled along the beach. We found an old boat that had been beached for awhile. It had a big hole in the side, and we crawled inside. We were laughing and talking when all of a sudden a bright light shined in on us and a man said, "Okay you two, get out of there right now!"

We were so scared we started to cry. He was from the Hawaiian police force. Our parents had called them and we were in trouble. He took us to a police car, and two officers drove us to the police station. They said they were going to call our parents.

I looked at Lana: "They are going to call Woody and Mom, and you are going to be in trouble too, all because I had to run away."

"Jane, tell the police what your stepfather is doing to you!"

I told them, "My stepfather is putting his hands all over my body and rubbing himself, and he is hurting me in my privates."

One of the policemen said, "Oh, my god!"

I thought maybe I could get him to put Woody in jail. But when Woody and Mom showed up, the cop said to them, "Your daughter said that you are touching her on her privates. Are you molesting this child?"

Woody said, "God, no! I love her! I'd never hurt her!"

Mom said, "Oh, she must be making it up. She makes up stuff all the time!"

I was crying and I told Mom, "He hurts me down there. I hate him, and I don't want to ever go home. Please, don't make me go home with him. He will really hurt me now. He told me he would kill me and you and Dick if I told anyone."

The policemen asked Woody, "You are in the marines, right?"

"Yes sir," Woody replied.

"We will have to send a report to your superior officer, and the marines will deal with you on this matter."

Then officer looked at Mom and said, "If you think your daughter is making up this story, you should get her some psychological help!"

"Okay, I will do that," Mom said as they stood up and shook hands. To the officer she said, "And thank you for finding my daughter."

"You're welcome, ma'am."

Then Mom looked at me: "Now go get in the car."

I ran to the officer and pleaded with him to keep me there so I wouldn't have to go with Mom and Woody. But he pulled me loose and said, "Your dad is a military man, and we can't do anything to him. But we will send a report, I promise! Now go home and be a good girl."

"I'll run away again, but next time no one will find me!" I cried. I ran to the car, where I found Dick in the back seat. I cried all the way home, and every time I looked up I could see Woody staring at me in the rear-view mirror. I knew he was going to kill me. I just knew it!

Mom said, "You better stop telling lies about your father. You know he takes good care of us, and we have a good life because of him. Now I don't want to hear this from you ever again!"

When we got home I ran to my bedroom and prayed to God to help me and protect me from Woody. I felt lost. I pulled the covers over my head in fear. I had told—and he might kill my mom, my brother, and me.

For nine years I had to put up with his hands, breath, and body touching mine, while I lay helpless with no one to defend me. I felt dirty, and as I grew older I knew it was wrong! But his threats instilled in me an enormous fear. The overwhelming reality of my life paralyzed me. Many times I had to make him think I liked what he did to me—simply, I thought, to survive. Until I met Lana, I had no one to turn to. I thought no one would believe me if I told, and I was right Now I didn't even have my best friend.

When morning came, I stayed in my room until everyone had gone. Sometime around noon, I ran over to Lana's house. Besides Lana, only the three youngest kids were there, in the kitchen with their mom. Lana was waiting for me in the yard. She said she had told her parents everything and that they felt sorry for me, but she was still in trouble for running away from home. I asked to talk to her mom, and Lana brought her outside. Her mom was kind and understanding and with open arms hugged me and said I could come to her anytime I needed help. I was so thankful to hear her say that. I needed an adult to believe me, and she did.

Mom arrived home around 4 P.M. She came into my bedroom and asked if I was all right. "Janie," she said, with a trace of understanding, "we're going to take you to a psychiatrist in a couple of days. Maybe we can get this all sorted out. The officer said it is the best thing to do."

After Mom left my room, I thought about how scary it would be to see a psychiatrist. But after awhile I thought the psychiatrist might help me understand why Woody had to do those things. And Mom might believe I was telling the truth.

Two weeks later, Woody received papers from his superior officer ordering him to attend counseling. Mom received papers from the police to take me to a psychiatrist. She drove me to Honolulu three days later. The child psychiatrist was a tender Hawaiian man with dark-brown eyes and coal-black hair. He showed me a bunch of black, abstract, ink spots and asked what it looked like to me. Some of the pictures looked like birds, fish, trees, and a picture that looked like me sitting on Woody's lap.

When he asked me whether I loved my mom and dad, I cried and said I loved my mom . . . and that I hated my stepfather because he touched my privates and wouldn't leave me alone.

Two hours later, my mom picked me up. She could see that my eyes were swollen. She gently put her hand on my leg and said she was sorry.

Later that evening I learned that the psychiatrist believed me, and he told Mom I was biting my nails because of all the stress over Woody. He said that this had been a traumatic experience and that I should have extended counseling.

I met with the psychiatrist two times a week for a month and at the end of the school season Woody received orders to return to El Toro Marine Base in California. I said goodbye to Lana, and she made me some flower leis to take with me on the ship. I'll never forget her.

We packed our things and boarded another military vessel for the long trip. When we got back to Tustin, California, Mom rented a 1950, three-bedroom house. One night Woody slugged Dick in the face in the garage. Then she got a full-time job with AT&T, kicked Woody out, and filed for a divorce.

I felt the weight of the world had been lifted from my shoulders! I was free from his at-least-weekly inspections. I could fall asleep knowing he was gone and that I didn't have to hide anymore. But I still had nightmares of him entering my room, and the hate stayed with me. Mom never sent me to another therapist, so I dealt with the nightmares as best as I could—by laughing and joking and trying to forget.

12

In June 1954, I was fourteen years old, and I spent a lot of time by myself. Mom was busy with new friends, and Dick had a steady summer job.

In July, Mom introduced me to the son of one of her friends, an up-and-coming army cadet at Camp San Luis Obispo, California. Soldiers who entered Officer Candidate School became junior officers in the California Army National Guard. Allen was an eighteen-year-old, clean-cut, six-foot four-inch gentleman, with a 1952 gold Cadillac Deville.

On our first date, Allen brought me flowers, escorted me to his car, and opened the door for me. He took me to a rodeo owned by his family, and we watched the show from behind the bullpens. He introduced me to the cowboys propped on the fence. When they pass around a bourbon bottle, I wanted to fit in and so took a few sips with the rest of them.

After the show Allen took me out to dinner. He pulled out my chair, waited for me to sit, and gently pushed my chair closer to the table. When I left the table to go to the rest room, he stood and helped me with my chair again. After dinner he took me to the local drive-in theater to watch a movie and smooch. Allen made me feel good—he treated me with respect. Soon he was taking me out every weekend.

After four more dates, our necking was getting a little heavier and he asked me whether I'd like to go to a motel.

"Yes," I said, in the heat of my excitement and a desire to experience lovemaking with a man I thought cared for me.

So Allen rented a room, and we took our clothes off and crawled into bed together. To my surprise, he pushed his penis inside me, got his jollies, and pulled out just as I was beginning to enjoy it. I was disappointed—I didn't experience anything like he did!

That September, I started seventh grade at Tustin Junior High in California, and Allen left for Camp San Luis Obispo. He wrote me almost every day, saying how we'd have a military wedding and live around the world. At school that year, the teachers complained to my mother about my use of Hawaiian slang, so she signed me up for charm school. There I learned to walk, sit, and eat "like a lady." I couldn't wait to practice my new manners on Allen when he returned at Christmas time.

One night at the drive-in theater, Allen whispered into my ear. "I love you, baby. I want to love you all the way."

"Let's go get a motel like we did before," I said, wanting to make him happy and hoping this time would be better for me, too.

We went to the same motel, and Allen undressed me. His hands were all over my body, and his mouth was in places it had never been before. All of a sudden, I became like a wild woman. I wanted him so much I was screaming for it. Allen gladly gave me his all. I knew I was supposed to love it, so I did, but after awhile it hurt a little, and I wanted him to stop. It was too late—he came inside me, and it was over. He pulled out and took off his rubber, then held me close. Afterwards, he took me home, kissed me good night, and drove away.

When I didn't hear from him right away, I began to worry that Allen didn't respect me anymore because I was easy. I'd learned that a proper lady plays hard to get. He said he loved me, and I wanted him to be in love with me. I had trusted him and given him what he wanted.

Several days later, the phone rang: "Baby, I miss you, and I want you again. Can I pick you up? Maybe we can go someplace."

I was relieved to hear his voice. "Yes, I'll be ready when you get here!"

When Allen came to pick me up, I suggested we go to my bedroom and make love. At the time, Mom had rented a cheaper place for us, and everything but our beds had been moved. She was spending most of her nights with a rich, married man, and my brother was usually with his girlfriend.

Allen followed me upstairs and started to undress me. I felt a bit shy about undressing in front of him, so I went into the bathroom to take off my clothes while he undressed in the bedroom. A few minutes later, I opened the door and saw him standing naked in front of the bed. I could see he was ready, and I watched him put on a rubber. I walked over to him, and we kissed and caressed each other until we fell onto my bed.

I know he wanted to make it nice for me, but his thrusting didn't feel good. I tried to look like I was enjoying it, but there were no bells or fireworks. In two or three minutes, it was over. Allen came, collapsed, and pulled out of me.

Suddenly, we heard car doors slam. I heard my mom's voice and the front door opening. I pushed Allen to the floor and ran to the bathroom, where I dressed as quickly as I could. Just as I pulled my blouse over my head, Mom walked into my bedroom.

"You little bitch!" she shouted. "Come out of that bathroom, you little whore!"

I opened the door and could see Allen standing next to the bed in his jockey shorts. His face was beaming red. Next, I saw my mom's boyfriend standing in the bedroom doorway. An attractive, middle-aged man, he sported a big grin, looking at me. Mom was to the right of the bathroom door, and when I stepped out, she grabbed my arm, spun me around, and threw me against the bedroom wall.

"You little bitch!" she said again. "I ought to beat you to death! What are you doing whoring around with this guy? I told you not to do things like this!"

"But, Mom, I love him, and he loves me! Mom, we . . . " I stammered. I was too embarrassed and afraid to say anything that made sense.

Mom turned to Allen. "Get the hell out! If I thought you would be screwing my daughter, I would never have introduced you to her. Now get your naked butt out of this house, and don't come back!"

Allen scooped up the rest of his clothes and, without even looking at me, walked out of the room and out the front door. I heard his car start, the tires squeal out of the driveway, and Allen riding out of my life forever.

Mom yelled some more; then we loaded the beds and moved to an apartment in Tustin. After we moved the beds inside, I stayed in my bedroom for the rest of the evening and cried my heart out. I wanted Allen to come and take me with him, but I knew I was too young.

I never saw him again; probably he was too scared to call me. I was crushed. Mom continued to remind me of my "downfall" for several few weeks, then finally stopped harassing me. I think she realized that my sleeping with boyfriends might get me married and out of the house.

In September 1955, I entered Tustin High School and became involved in after-school sports. I joined the girl's field hockey team and also participated in softball and swimming. Being on the teams was a great way for me to meet new friends.

I also joined Tustin High's Pep Club and met a new boyfriend, Jim Bogady. He was a five-foot-six, solid Italian knockout! I just couldn't resist this cute senior—the most valuable baseball player and the captain of the football and baseball teams to boot. Jim thought I was something too, and when homecoming week approached, he insisted I run for homecoming court. I was crowned princess of my class.

Soon everyone knew we were a couple. Jim picked me up in a brand new, blue-and-white Chevrolet. We hung out with other couples at the Tustin Drive-in and made out like everyone else. I let Jim explore my breasts a little, but I pushed his hand away when he stayed there too long or squeezed too hard. I played the innocent girl I still thought I was, and he controlled himself for a time. After awhile, though, we were going all the way. Sometimes my skin stuck to the seat cover, and Jim had to peel me off the seat when we were through.

By this time, I was beginning to enjoy sex, and the fact that I had a big guy at school added to my enjoyment. Jim was a little guy, but he knew how to make me feel good. After a few months, we "graduated" to motels—both in Tustin and Anaheim. Mom never questioned me about where I was. She liked it that I was with a popular and successful boyfriend. I think she hoped he would marry me and take me away.

In the fall of 1955—November 8 to be exact—Mom's divorce had become final, and Woody had to start paying her $225 alimony per month. After school was out the following spring, she moved us to yet another apartment in Anaheim. Over a garage, the apartment had a huge deck, where we could suntan and she could throw parties.

On certain occasions, Mom asked me to stay at a friend's for the night so that she could entertain her friends. I think she was trying to hide the fact that she had a daughter who had turned fifteen at the end of March. I helped her maintain her masquerade by doing as she asked. Dick graduated from Tustin High in June 1956, enlisted in the U.S. Air Force, and was sent to Texas for boot camp. So I was the only one left to interfere with her life.

After I moved to Anaheim, Jim and I drifted apart. We had cared for each other, but we weren't in love. I started my sophomore year at Anaheim High School where, once again, I had to make new friends. During the first week of school I met the girl who became my longest and best friend, Carol.

"Why, you're just a shrimp!" was the first thing she said to me. She was almost six feet tall, and I was only a few inches over five feet. She was a friendly giant, and I was Jack at the bottom of the beanstalk. Carol even bent over to talk to me, which at first made me uncomfortable. But she was a great listener, and soon I knew she did that only because she wanted to hear every word I said.

Carol and I met for the first time one evening outside a building at Anaheim High, where both of us had come for a class in nurse's training. The teacher was late, which gave us a few minutes to get acquainted. We were hardly ever apart after that.

Carol was a senior in high school, two years older than I. Most of my friends have been older; I seemed to relate more easily to people who were more experienced—perhaps I've thought they would be wiser and keep me safe. Carol had a loving family, something I didn't. Her mother and father instantly took me in, and I was often at her house when Mom was going out to bars with her friends or was having parties at the apartment.

I was fortunate to find Carol when I did because Mom was beginning to show signs that she didn't want me around. "You're always eating," she said to me one day when I was having an after-school snack. "You always eat up all the food around here, and I'm going to put a stop to it." Then Mom had a bar with a lock on it welded to the refrigerator door, and she kept the key.

From that time on, Mom fed me only when she and I were home at the same time, sometimes after she got home from one of her nights with her friends at the bars. When I got hungry, I went to Carol's house or went without.

As Mom became more irresponsible, she began asking other people to take care of me. Soon after she met Carol, Mom called her parents and asked for me to stay with them while she went on a vacation with her rich boyfriend. Carol's mom said, "Sure, we always have a houseful of kids, and one more won't make a difference." With six children already in their family, she and her gem of a husband accepted me with no reservations.

Mom began to ignore me even when we were together. She went into her bedroom after fixing a meal or coming home from a party and shut the door without speaking to me. Even when I spoke to her, she only half-listened, offering only "uh-huh" or a grunt in response. Despite her attitude, I loved my mother and wanted her to love me. I tried to be a good girl, not to complain or make her angry, but she refused to notice me. I pursued her, but nothing I did changed the way she treated me.

I began to feel like a burden, unwanted, and I started to look for someone to notice and love me. The one I chose was Bob Harvey.

13

Starting over, this time at Anaheim High, was difficult. I'd lost interest in sports, and my mother couldn't have cared less whether I succeeded in school. So I decided to hang around with Carol and have some fun.

Carol and I signed up for the nurses' training classes at West Fullerton Community Hospital. I really enjoyed medicine, and I assumed we could use what we learned from it to make a living. After awhile, we began skipping school, about once a week. Carol's boyfriend, Curly, drove us to the Pike, an amusement park in Long Beach, where we met marines and sailors who tried to get us drunk on beer.

One day, Carol and I met Curly at his house, and we all went to pick up his friend Bob. When Bob got into the car in his white navy uniform, I thought my heart was going to stop! He was five-feet-ten-inches tall with blond hair cut full on top and short on the sides, emphasizing the biggest pair of dark brown eyes with the longest eyelashes I'd ever seen.

"And who is this?" Bob asked Curly with a great smile, as he snuggled into the back seat beside me. "Are you my date, or am I just dreaming?" he said, turning and looking into my eyes. "You're beautiful." That's all it took. I was instantly in love.

Instead of going to the beach, Curly drove us to an orange grove near Anaheim to park. While Carol and Curly made out in the front seat, Bob and I talked for a few minutes, and then he kissed and hugged me for nearly an hour before he had to return to his base in Long Beach. I didn't want to let him go.

I couldn't wait to see Bob again, and in three weeks we were back together. Carol, Curly, Bob, and I went to Newport Beach. The minute Bob got into the back seat we started making out. When we reached the beach, we took a walk down the sand and found a spot all to ourselves. He held me close, and I could feel his heart pounding. Nothing could tear me away.

That afternoon, Bob said, "I can't stand this any longer. I want you, and I want to be with you. Will you go with me to a place where we can be alone?"

"Yes," I said.

He took me to a nearby motel, where we made love. I acted innocent, as I had with Allen and Jim, but this time I felt I was "in love." He was gentle, considerate, and romantic. He seemed to care for me as much as I did for him, and when he made love to me, the bells chimed—at least I could hear them tinkling. Another time we made love below the cliffs north of Huntington Beach, behind a clump of bushes and mounds of sand. It was romantic to be outside, hearing the waves, watching the stars. We got a lot of sand on ourselves and had fun taking a dip to wash it off.

On April 1, 1957, Bob asked Mom, in my presence, whether he could marry me in June. My mother laughed, "Oh, can't you make it sooner?" Then, "Don't you think you're a little young to get married?"

I grabbed Bob's arm: "But Mom, I love him and he loves me."

"Don't you think it would be a good idea to wait two years?" Mom looked concerned, "I mean, honey, you just turned sixteen."

Bob intervened: "But she's real mature for her age."

"Yes, I agree," Mom said.

"I don't think I could ever feel this way about anybody else because of what Woody did to me," I pleaded.

Bob held my hand and said, "I love Janie, and I will protect her and never let anything happen to her again."

Mom looked at the floor and said, finally, "I'll have to go to the school and talk to the principal."

Bob eyes lit up. "Does that mean okay? Does that mean we have your blessing?"

Mom looked at us, serious: "Don't you guys go making a bunch of babies, and then come back to me . . . because you know if you make your bed, you lie in it! Do you understand what I'm saying?"

We just nodded. The next day Bob went back to his ship in Long Beach, and I went back to school. A few days later Mom and I went to see the principal. He agreed I was mature for my age, and after I left the room the two of them continued to talk.

Getting approval from Bob's mother, Mae Keck, was not so easy. She had been divorced and remarried, and she said we were both too young; the idea was ridiculous. But Bob kept telling her how much he loved me, and finally she went along with it, wishing us love, luck, and happiness.

I thought my life would be wonderful. I loved a man who loved me, and I thought we'd live on a military base like the one I grew up on. I wanted my children to have a stable and secure life with lots of love and happiness. I couldn't wait for my dream to come true.

Bob and I were married on June 5, 1957. Our wedding was wonderful: more than forty relatives and friends attended the ceremony at the Wishing Well Chapel in Anaheim, California. Mom paid for the wedding, and I wore a gorgeous, low-cut, white dress with a long skirt full with crinolines. A small net veil sat delicately on my hair, curled on top and swept back on the sides. Bob wore a black tuxedo and was more handsome than ever. He was eighteen years old, and I was still sixteen.

We had a short reception, and Mom handed me a card containing a hundred-dollar bill. Then Carol and Curly took Bob and me to the Fullerton train station; we were headed to Seattle, Washington. There, we found the navy shipyard at the waterfront near the downtown. Bob checked in, and we walked all over downtown trying to find a place to live. Bob was only a deuce (private)—the navy didn't provide housing for the families of its lowest rank.

Finally, out of frustration and because it was the only thing we could afford, we rented a room in a dark, dingy, rundown hotel on Main Street. We paid the twenty-dollar weekly rent for five weeks in advance, spending our wedding present.

Bob had tried to save, but there wouldn't be much to live on. We were simply young and happily in love. After paying the landlord, Bob picked me up and carried me over the threshold. I didn't care whether we were lying on a rock as long as we were together. He carried me to the bed, and that's where we stayed until the next morning.

Our room was just that, one room. The bathroom was down the hall, and everyone on the floor shared it. One window overlooked Main Street, occupied by drunken sailors, prostitutes, and thieves. Bob and I ate our meals on a tiny end table that barely held two plates. There was no refrigerator, so we had to buy food every day. When Bob brought me a two-burner hotplate, I was thrilled that I could heat canned foods and fry up meals in the room.

I'll never forget that street. I was afraid to open the door or go to the store. Bob had to knock three times and yell "Pie face!" so I could be sure it was him. When he went to sea for weeks or months at a time, I stayed in the room and just sat on the windowsill and watched the people going up and down the street. I was so lonesome, and I asked myself "What have I done?" many times. I had dropped out of school, I had no money, and I had nothing to do. Each month I waited for Bob's paycheck, at first $98.17 a month. After two months and a raise he got $119.34 per month. After the rent was paid, we had $39.34 for everything else.

I had thought we'd have a nice place to live and have a family. But I'd fallen in love with a guy with no money, and on top of that I was alone for up to three months at a time. I tried a job at a suitcase factory, but after working full time for four weeks, I was laid off. Still, when Bob came home and held me, I forgot the depressing times. And I knew better than to complain about loneliness—a military wife never made it hard for her husband to serve our country.

After his first trip, Bob returned home with a shipmate named Freddy. He was a tall, skinny drink of water with blond hair and blue eyes. Bob told me Freddy would be living with us, and that afternoon we looked for a bigger apartment. The next day we moved into a furnished one-bedroom place with a full kitchen and a small living room with a couch. I was happy to get out of that scary neighborhood, and now I could cook for my husband and Freddy.

At first, it was fun listening to Bob and Freddy when they drank beer and talked about the navy. Bob liked me to sit on his lap; he cuddled and pinched me just to see me laugh. Then he started inviting more buddies home from the ship. For awhile I smiled and laughed because I loved Bob and wanted to make him proud of his wife. But after awhile, the partying was driving me crazy. I told Bob I couldn't live that way any longer.

The next week we moved to an efficiency apartment in a nicer neighborhood—and started work on having a baby. A couple of weeks later, Bob went to sea again. During that time I missed my period and thought I was pregnant. But it was a false alarm—the doctor at the navy clinic said I wanted a baby so much that I had made my period stop.

When Bob returned home, he laughed. "Well, you know how much fun it is to try."

When Bob went out on another cruise, I missed my period again, and this time I really was pregnant. I sat right down and wrote to tell him he was going be a father.

Before my letter reached the ship, I got a letter from him: "Dear Jane, I'll be coming home in two days. We need to talk. I have met a girl in Iceland. I'll be picking up my belongings when I get home. I'm sorry."

I was devastated. How could he do this? All my dreams were crushed. For the next two days I watched for him out the kitchen window. Finally on the second afternoon, I heard a car pull up to the curb. Bob emerged from a black Ford piled high with gear and full of servicemen.

He knocked on the door, using our secret knock, and I opened the door. "I'm back," he shouted, handing me a beautiful floral scarf, a bouquet of flowers, and a red silk dress.

I just stood there, looking at him, and sobbing.

"Oh, baby, I love you so much," he said. He put his arm around me, steered me into the bedroom, and sat me down on the bed. "Can you ever find it in your heart to forgive me? I made a mistake. Please, please, forgive me."

I couldn't move and I kept on crying. Finally I gulped, "You broke my heart."

He said the girl in Iceland was too old for him and that she had led him to believe she loved him. All she wanted was sex, he said, and they didn't do anything. I didn't believe him. He moved closer, put his arms around me, and lay me down on the bed. He kissed me on my neck and mouth.

"I need you, honey," Bob said. "I've been away from you for so long, and I need you to love me." He kissed me some more and I began to feel myself giving in to him.

"I never loved anyone else but you, honey," he said, and I began to believe it.

I loved him so much, and it was wonderful to be back in his arms. I could feel myself wanting him too. My heart turned to mush, and I forgave him. After we made love, I told him about our baby.

"A baby?" he cried. Are you sure this time?"

"Yes. The doctor said I'll deliver in the first week of June, which will be our first-year anniversary.

We spent the rest of his leave looking for an apartment in Seattle with a playground for our baby. The one we found was a small one-bedroom, with a living room and kitchen. Now I thought I could be a real housewife and mother-to-be. I could cook and clean and raise our baby just as I had always wanted.

When Bob went to sea, I decided to get a baby-sitting job, so I could buy some things for the baby. At the Laundromat down the street, I saw an ad: "Baby-sitter wanted for two small children. Rates negotiable." I ran to the pay phone and dialed the number.

With that call, I got my second job, baby-sitting for a young couple living in a new house in the Queen Anne section of Seattle. I sat for them a few times, and they began calling me on a regular basis, especially on weekends. I was happy to work and to make some money for baby things.

One Friday night, the mother picked me up and drove me to her house to baby-sit. After she and her husband left the house, I tucked the two children in for the night and enjoyed the luxury of their beautiful home. I thought, "Someday, I'll be living in a house like this with Bob and our kids. We'll be just as happy as this family, happier even."

At about 1 A.M., the couple came home. They left their car at the bar because they'd been drinking. A man named Buck had volunteered to drive them home and said he'd drive me home too. As he drove, Buck told me he was a marine. We started talking, and he said, "I think you are so beautiful."

"Thank you," I replied.

"Have you ever been married?" Buck asked.

"I am married," I said.

"You are? Are you married to a real man?"

"Of course, I'm married to a real man. He's in the navy," I said proudly.

"Navy men are nothing but pussies."

"He's no pussy; he's a man! And I don't like you to say that about my husband.

Buck looked at the maternity top I was wearing over my pedal pushers: "Are you pregnant?"

"Yes," I said.

"I don't believe you're pregnant."

Before I realized what he was doing, he turned the car left into an alley and parked behind a gas station. Now he was scaring me, and I remembered what Mom had told me in case I ever thought I was going to be raped: "Try to talk him out of it."

I tried. My heart pounded. Trembling all over, I managed to say, "You don't want to do this, Buck. I'm going to have a baby. Think what this could do to it."

He didn't listen but put his hand on my leg and scooted across the seat toward me. He had a terrible look on his face. "You're too pretty and young to be pregnant. You're going to feel what a real man is like."

"Oh, please don't do this," I pleaded as he unzipped his pants.

He grabbed my hand and put it on his penis. Lurching towards me he grabbed one breast, then pulled on the neck of my maternity blouse so hard it split down the middle, bursting off the buttons. He pitched my blouse into the back seat. Then he pinned one arm behind my back and pushed me up against the seat so that he could get at my neck and face. He kissed me on the mouth, and I could feel the sticky trails of his slobber on my cheeks and throat as his mouth moved down toward my chest. He flipped my bra off with one move, licking and nuzzling as he moved down between my breasts. He sucked on one, then the other, chewing harder and harder from the bottom toward the nipple. I could feel his teeth clamp down. There was a searing pain as he bit hard into my flesh.

I tried to resist, but I couldn't make a sound. My throat, my whole body, seemed paralyzed. I could see Woody in his face and feel Woody in his hands, and I was powerless to stop him.

The next thing I knew, Buck was holding a pocketknife to my throat.

"Okay! Okay!" I tried to scream. "Just let go of my arm and I will." He let go of my arm, and I reached behind to undo the zipper of my pedal pushers.

Buck stuck the knife under my chin. "Take them down! Take them down!" he ordered.

Sobbing, I pulled my pants down around my thighs, but I couldn't get them to go any farther. He pinned both arms behind me, so I could barely move. Still holding the knife under my chin, he grabbed at the elastic waist of my panties and, in one jerk, ripped them in half, tearing them off. Entirely exposed, I kicked wildly at the dashboard, at the front window, at anything my legs could reach. Buck put the knife to my stomach. I stopped kicking and sat, my arms pinned behind me.

"My baby's in there! My baby's in there. Please don't hurt me there!" I sobbed. "I'll do it if you just don't hurt my baby."

"Then shut up and enjoy it," Buck said.

I stopped crying; my body went numb. Buck pushed me down on the seat, pulled off my pedal pushers, and raised my legs over my head. He pinned me to the front seat with the weight of his body, leaning on me so hard that my knees were almost touching the seat. When he penetrated, the pain was so terrible I bit my lip. I could taste the blood from the cut, but the only thing I could think of was my baby.

Buck pounded into me like some kind of wild animal for several minutes before exploding inside me, grunting and gasping as he shot his "real man" into this captive, pregnant navy wife. When it was over, he zipped up his pants, reached over and opened the door, and shouted, "Get out of the car, you little whore."

I scrunched out from under him and slid, backwards, onto the ground. I saw him drop the knife on the floor near the gas pedal. He picked up my pants, bra, and panties from the floor, reached into the back seat for my blouse, and tossed the clothes at me. Then he spit on me. He pulled the car door shut from where he was sitting, started the car, backed up, and took off.

For a few minutes, all I could do was cry and shake. Not only had I just been humiliated and raped, I was also stranded in a part of the city I didn't recognize. My clothes were in shreds, and I had no money but a little change. I had to find help.

I saw a light in the window of a house about a block away and headed for it. I pounded on the door until an elderly woman opened the door.

"I've been raped! I've been raped! Call the police. Please, call the police!" I said.

"Oh, dear, you look like you've had quite a beating," she said. "Charlie, come and help the poor girl."

Her husband came to the door and helped me into the house, while she ran to phone the police. My legs were bruised, my stomach was sore, and my clothes were torn. The police came and took me to the station. A woman police officer took pictures of my legs, shoulder, and stomach. Then she took me into a room and tried to calm me.

I explained what had happened, and the police called the people I had been baby-sitting for. They said they didn't know the guy, that they'd just happened to meet him at the bar and that he'd offered them a ride home. The police officer took me back to our apartment.

Bob came back to Seattle several weeks later, and almost before we embraced and said hello I blurted out that I had been raped.

"That son of a bitch! I'll kill him! Where is he?"

"I don't know," I said, tears rolling down my face.

"What do you mean, you don't know?"

"He was a stranger. I thought he was a friend of the people I baby-sat for because he brought them home from the bar."

Bob turned on me. "You fucking little whore, you probably wanted it. You little bitch! You think you're so cute and sexy all the time. You probably asked for it."

He had never said anything like this to me before, and my heart broke. How could a man who loved me say such things? The hurt I felt that night stayed with me for months. I never really forgot it, but I put it aside so that Bob and I could be happy as we awaited the birth of our baby.

Cindy Lou, our first daughter, was born in Seattle on June 3, 1958. Her skin was like Bob's, an olive color, and she had dark brown eyes. Bob was part Chippewa, and she inherited the features of an Indian princess. After she was born, Bob held me and looked at Cindy with tears rolling down his cheeks. He called his mother right away, to tell her about our wonderful baby. When, in the following months, I talked with Mae or my mother by phone, they seemed as thrilled as we were. Bob and I agreed Cindy was beautiful.

From the day I brought Cindy home, Bob and I lay beside her on the bed and gazed at her with disbelief. She smelled so fresh and new. Her round face and baby-fat body were perfect in every way. We were amazed at the strength in her little hand as she squeezed my finger. When we tickled her soft tummy she smiled, cooed, or laughed out loud. The hospital gave us some soft cotton diapers, which I washed out in the bathroom toilet and air-dried on the edge of the tub.

At first I was nervous about bathing her. I made sure the water in the kitchen sink wasn't too hot or cold. I carefully held her head as I gently washed her. She loved to kick and splash, often soaking the front part of my blouse. I dried her with a soft towel and doused her bottom with baby powder before putting on her tiny diaper and wrapping her in a blanket. We didn't have a crib, so I put her on the bed, surrounded by pillows so she wouldn't fall off.

Cindy made me happy. The minute she woke, she cried for food and a diaper change. She never went hungry, and I never let her sit and play in a dirty diaper like Filthy McNasty's mom had done. I promised I'd never let anyone come into her bedroom and hurt her. "I'll watch over you forever," I whispered in her ear.

Bob was happy, too. He held her and made her giggle and told her how much he'd miss her when he had to go out to sea again. But he left us for another three-months' duty without enough money to feed Cindy and me.

I didn't know what to do, and about that time I met a neighbor who suggested she teach me the art of shoplifting. First, she had me rent a freezer. Then my new "friend" and I went to the supermarket wearing big, loose coats. We stole steaks and hamburger by sticking them under our arms, into our pockets, and into Cindy's stroller. At first, I was scared and felt guilty about stealing, but then I became a pro. When Bob came home, I showed him our stocked freezer, and when he asked me how I did it, I told him the truth.

"Good going," was all he said. My life of crime (that one anyway) ended a few months later when Bob got out of the navy and we moved back to southern California.

Our new home in Santa Ana was a one-bedroom trailer. Bob did not find a job for several weeks, and when he did, he lost it because of staying out the night before and arriving late to work in the morning. In fact, he never kept a job after he got out of the military. All he wanted to do was get high with his friends. Whenever he had money, he spent it on pot, pills, or alcohol.

Eventually I went to Bob's mother, Mae, to ask her for help. I told her Bob couldn't hold a job and that we needed to borrow for our rent as well. Blind to Bob's faults, Mae didn't believe me. Just about this time I became pregnant with our second child, so I was also worried that we had no medical insurance.

Bob didn't seem to care. After I told him I had had enough of his partying, he slowed his daily merrymaking for baby Cindy and me. But he still couldn't hold a job.

Roberta Jane was born on February 5, 1960, at Santa Ana Community Hospital. She was a beautiful bald-headed child with red lips and soft skin. She looked just like me when I was a baby. Bob and I held her in our arms, and we were so happy. She was perfect in every way.

I was happy to have another little girl, but I was hardly more than a child (a month short of nineteen) myself. I stressed out from 24-hour duty with two little ones—an active toddler and a baby who cried constantly because I had a breast infection and there just wasn't enough milk.

Finally, I went to stay with my mom in Anaheim for a week. She helped me with Roberta, and every day Bob dropped Cindy at Mae's so that he could look for work. At the end of the day Bob picked up Cindy, came to see Roberta and me, ate supper, and returned with Cindy to our apartment.

Bob did get a job at a liquor store, but after two weeks he was fired. I got a nurse's aide job at Fullerton Community Hospital. For once we were able to pay the bills, with a little money leftover for the girls. Eventually we moved to Anaheim and the same apartment complex as Curly and Carol, who by that time had married.

After a few months, things went sour and Bob lost his job and started partying again, this time with Carol and Curly and their friends. When I was with them, he flirted right in front of me with other women, no matter where we were.

One night after work I walked across the street to Carol's apartment to borrow a baking pan, and right in front of her apartment door, I saw Bob kissing another woman. That was it. I stormed over, slapped him across the face, told him it was over and that I wanted a divorce. I returned to our apartment, packed some of the girls' clothes, gathered up Cindy and Roberta, and went to stay with a friend in Long Beach.

Two days later she brought us back to the apartment. Bob had taken his clothes and the car and gone. I found a baby-sitter and walked the eight miles (each way) to work. I couldn't afford the rent and the sitter too, and after a few weeks, I called Bob's mother. Mae said she didn't know where her son was, and when I asked her to lend me enough money to keep the apartment, she said all she could do was keep the girls until I found an affordable place.

The next morning the baby-sitter said she needed more money to continue, and I didn't have it. I had to take care of my girls, and so I lost my job.

14

So Bob's lack of a steady job, his drinking, popping pills, and cheating led me to file for divorce, in August 1960. I wanted my children and I needed legal help, so I looked in the yellow pages, called one of the numbers, and a secretary put me through to a divorce attorney. I told him about my problems and what I wanted him to do. He said his office was near the Disneyland Hotel and that I should meet him in the lounge at noon the next day.

Then I called Bob's mother, Mae, to watch the girls. She asked what had happened, and I said we had a bad fight and I caught him kissing another woman.

"Oh, it will blow over. Everything will be okay," she said.

"No, not this time. I'm done with him not working and not being responsible."

The next morning Mae drove over to pick up the girls. Then I put on a nice, white cotton dress and took a bus to the hotel. At the lounge I had to ask each of several men whether he was the attorney.

Finally, a man waved to me from the end of the bar. He was at least thirty years older than I, with receding gray-streaked black hair, a mustache, thick black eyebrows, wire-rimmed glasses, and a tanned face. He wore a tailored, navy-pinstriped, double-breasted suit and big diamonds on each hand. He ordered a soft drink for me in a deep, commanding voice.

As I told him my story, I noticed him staring at my breasts. He seemed more interested in the area below my neck than in what was happening in my life. I ignored it. After a couple of drinks, he moved closer to me, holding my hand while I cried, eventually touching my leg with his.

When the subject of his fee came up, I said I would not be able to pay him until I reached a settlement with Bob regarding child support and alimony. He winked, began to rub my back, and said, "Well, honey, we could take it out in trade."

I didn't know what "take it out in trade" meant.

He moved closer, looking into my eyes, and said, "You know what I mean."

I backed away: "No, I don't know what you mean."

"Well, let's go upstairs, and I'll show you."

Now realizing what he implied, I retorted, "You'll get your money, but it will be winter in hell before I'll go to bed with you!" I shoved my stool back, slid my glass towards his, stormed from the bar, and took a bus back to the apartment.

There I found an eviction notice taped to the door. We owed two months' rent; if I didn't pay it by the end of the week, I'd be out. I was scared; I could think about only one thing at a time. I called Mae, and she brought the girls back to the apartment.

When Mae arrived, I told her about the notice, saying I had no money for rent because Bob couldn't keep a job. I explained that I had been taking care of the girls during the day while Bob "looked for work." At night Bob had watched the girls while I worked the second shift at the hospital. But with him gone, I had no one to watch the girls. I couldn't afford a sitter, so had to quit my job to take care of them.

"Have you heard from Bob?" she asked.

"No, I haven't."

"Bob is just like his dad. You know, Bob's dad left me right after Bob was born, and I never saw him again."

"Yes. He told me you had to take care of the three children alone before you married Clarence."

"I have to go. I'll call you tomorrow."

I got the girls ready for bed and read *The Three Bears*. They always laughed when I growled for the bears in the story. Sitting there, reading to them, I thought how I would have to let them stay with Mae and Clarence while I looked for work and a place to live.

The only other thing I could think of was that the church down the street might help me. I hadn't attended services there, but Mom had taken Dick and me to a Lutheran church on Sundays. Also Carol and I had sung in a church choir and attended summer church camp. A church would help someone in trouble. We could easily walk there; someone there would help us.

So we walked. I carried six-month-old Roberta in my arms, holding Cindy's hand in mine. We climbed the stairs to the church door, but when I pulled on the door, it wouldn't open. It was locked and there was nobody around. I sat on the stairs and cried. Then Cindy started to cry, then Roberta. I felt my heart stop. I'd never felt so helpless. I had no choice but to trust Mae to care for my children until I found a new place to live.

We walked back to the apartment. I ripped the eviction notice from the door and threw it to the floor. Inside, I gave Roberta a bottle and fed Cindy. Then I called Mae and told her she could come and pick them up in the morning. As I started to cry, Mae said, "Don't worry. I'll take good care of them. Everything will be fine."

So I put Cindy's little shorts, shirts, and shoes and Roberta's pacifier, diapers, dish, and spoon into a paper bag. I lay on the bed with the girls, holding them close, holding back my tears. I wanted to be strong. But my heart sank when I saw Mae approaching the apartment the next day.

I talked with her a few minutes until she said, "Well, we better get on with this."

I walked down the stairs with Roberta in my arms, holding Cindy's hand, and I put them in the backseat of Mae's car. I can still see Cindy looking out the back window as they drove off. I waved and blew a kiss. We waved to each other until they disappeared. I went back to the apartment, threw myself onto the bed, and bawled.

A few hours later I went to see Carol. When I returned, the door to the apartment was padlocked. I couldn't get my clothes or any of my belongings. I headed on foot to Mom and her boyfriend's new house, six miles away, thinking about what I could do.

A friend once told me that her sister worked in Hollywood as a cocktail waitress, making three hundred dollars a day in tips. Curly had gotten me a fake driver's license saying I was twenty-one, so I figured I could go to Hollywood, get a job like that, and soon afford a place for my daughters and me.

But I had to get there first. I needed money for a train ticket and something nice to wear that made me look like I was at least twenty-one years old.

When I reached the house, I smashed a pane of glass in the back door, headed straight to Mom's bedroom closet, and pulled out a black dinner dress. It was a size seven, and I was about an eight, so it fit really tight. I put on black-lace nylons and high-heels, combed my hair, covered my face with makeup, and inspected myself in the full-length mirror. "It works," I thought. "Nobody can tell I'm not twenty-one!"

Then I scavenged through the house for money. I looked in every closet, every drawer, every jar, and took every penny I found. In the bedroom, I found a coin collection and poured the change into a shiny black clutch purse. I inspected myself in the mirror again and decided I was taking control of my life. Whatever hit me next, I was going to be ready!

I called Carol and asked her to take me to the Union Pacific station in Fullerton, so I could get a ticket for Hollywood. I needed to get a job, and when I had some money, I'd be back for the girls. I told her that Bob's mother was going to help with the girls while I was gone. On the way to Fullerton, Carol tried to persuade me to stay with her and Curly, but they had only a one-bedroom apartment, and I'd made up my mind. I was sure I could get a job in Hollywood.

"Oh, my God, Jane, you better not go there," she said. "You don't know anyone there."

I'll be okay. I have to do this for my girls."

At the station, I bought a ticket, and just before boarding I promised Carol I'd call her as soon as I got a room. Once at Union Station in Hollywood, I caught a cab—just as if I knew what I was doing: "Take me to Sunset Boulevard."

During the ride I thought about how all the men in cars had honked their horns and stared at me as I walked to Fullerton Community Hospital every day, where I'd earned just $1.15 per hour. They seemed to stare through my clothes. It was degrading. I thought about trying to find a decent job, how some good guy might fall in love with me, one who had a home where I could raise my girls. I believed God would show me the way and everything would work out for the best.

The cab driver let me out on Sunset Boulevard. I paid him from the coin collection and got a room at a motel for the night. After a short rest, I showered, put on Mom's black dress again, and walked down Sunset Boulevard past Schwab's Drugstore, where Lana Turner had been discovered. I kept going, around the corner, to a cocktail lounge called Sherrie's.

I sauntered into the bar as if I knew what I was doing and took a seat. I must have stood out from the crowd in my black dinner dress and furry sweater. The bartender looked at my fake driver's license and served me a drink. Soon several men in the bar offered to replenish it, and in no time, I got a little tight.

After awhile, I noticed a good-looking man dressed in a suit, sitting at the end of the bar and watching me in the mirror. After I became aware of his staring, he smiled and winked and bought me a drink. Finally, he walked over and said, "You sure are a pretty little thing. How old are you?"

"Eighteen," I replied fuzzily.

"You're just barely eighteen, aren't you?"

"Yeah," I said.

"Well, honey, you are just a beautiful girl." He sat down next to me, saying his name was Tyler Wilson. He was in his early thirties, nearly six feet tall, slim and athletic. His dishwater-blond hair was slicked back on both sides of his face. A slight wave in front accented his blue eyes and square jaw.

I wasn't used to drinking, and I had had way too much. I was laughing and giggling like the teenager I was.

"Come on up to my place, and I'll make you something to eat," Tyler invited. I was hungry.

At his apartment, Tyler fixed me a sandwich and made small talk until he had me where he wanted me—in bed. Afterwards, he said I was the wildest gal he'd ever been with, and I told him about my dilemma.

"Well, if you really want some help, I can connect you up with some people who can pay you cash for your services," he said.

"Great. What do I have to do?"

"My father and I run a car lot and could put you up in a room for a week, about seven miles away. I know quite a few fellows who would spend good money to be with you for a few minutes."

"What do you mean—'be with me'?"

"Well, they'll give you some money for a roll in the hay."

"No way! I'd never do anything like that. Are you kidding?"

"Do you want to make some money, or do you *not* want to make some money?"

I hesitated. I thought about having not much more than the clothes on my back. I had barely enough money to last the week, and I needed to do something fast.

"Okay." I started to cry. "I guess I might be able to do that." My heart was pounding so hard I thought I was going to be sick.

"Oh, honey, you'll be able to do it. Hell, men will do anything to be with a girl as pretty as you are, who knows what she's doing in bed. You won't have any problem making fast cash! Believe me, those guys will be knocking your door down!"

"What do I do?" I asked.

"I'll tell the guys at work how great you are in bed, and I'll call to let you know who's coming. You can put on something sexy before he gets there. When the man gets inside the room, ask him what he wants. Then make him give you cash up front before you do anything. Hell, a man will gladly give you fifteen or twenty bucks just to look at you for a few minutes."

I felt myself giving in. "What do I do with them?"

"After the man pays you, you take him into the bathroom and wash his dick with cool, soapy water and check to see if he's got any sexual diseases. But remember, don't wash him too good, or he'll get his rocks off before you have a chance to earn your money."

"Okay, Tyler, I'll try it. But only until I find a job."

The next day Tyler moved me into the Sunset Plaza Hotel and told his buddies about me. He called to tell me that a fellow salesman would visit me at 5 P.M. I put on my mother's black dress and waited for him to arrive.

When the man knocked on the door, I opened it. I was nervous but relieved to find that, as Tyler had said, he was a clean-cut man in his early thirties. I could tell he liked the way I looked as his eyes scanned over my body. I asked him what he wanted, and he said, "I'd like a blow job."

"Could you pay me twenty bucks for that?" I asked, trying to be "professional." My heart pounded.

He saw that I was scared and said, "Yes. Are you going to be okay?"

"I've never done anything like this before."

The man pulled out his wallet and handed me a twenty.

I was so excited to see that money: "Thank you. First I have to wash you up!"

I took him to the bathroom, gently inspected his privates for disease, and washed his penis, carefully to avoid arousal. He led me to the bed, saying," Just try to relax, and it will be okay." I sat him down on the bed, and he came right away. He thanked me, put on his pants and tie, and was gone.

After he closed the door, I thought, "Oh my God, what have I done?" I felt sick and started to cry. Then I got down on my knees and prayed to God to help me out of the mess I was in. After regaining my calm, I wondered why this married man with a family wanted to go to bed with a stranger. I could be the same age as his daughter or son! For my part, I felt sick when I thought of it.

Still, I needed the money, and an hour later another man came to my door. He was older and reminded me of my stepfather. He was dressed in a suit and wanted straight sex. I *asked* for money—because I was still scared and desperate for cash. I washed him up, took off my nylons, and did the job. He thanked me with a fifteen-dollar tip, dressed, and left the room.

These men acted as if they'd just gone through a carwash. In and out, then home to the wife and kids, the loving family man. They had no connection to me, and when I counted up the money I had earned in less then an hour, I didn't care. I didn't like the work, but the money was great. "Lots of people live this way," I rationalized. And pretty soon, I was earning two hundred dollars in one afternoon!

I was of two minds about what I was doing. In the moments I felt dirty and degraded, I reminded myself that if I made a lot of money, I could go get my girls. Whenever I started to hate myself, I counted the money again, blocking out how I had earned it. I had to have enough to get an apartment. I would do whatever it took to get the girls back. I even thought of how I was putting the welfare of the children above my own pride.

I was so naïve that I didn't see any of this as abuse—not by the men or myself— of me. But in reality, I was a misguided nineteen-year-old, selling my body to complete strangers.

After about three days, Tyler came to my room and told me all the men had called to say I was a beautiful girl who had pleased them. We lay on the bed to cuddle as I told him about my day. He was aroused immediately, and he made love to me with a passion I'd never seen in Bob or anyone else. He said I was what every man on earth would want and that I should be making lots of money every day. That's the last thing I heard as I fell asleep.

The next day, three weeks after I'd left, I took the train back to Anaheim, using the money I'd earned three days before, which I had split fifty-fifty with Tyler. I had just a little under a hundred dollars in my purse when I got off the train in Fullerton. I was determined to get my girls back and start again.

I took a cab to Mae's home in Anaheim. She was home, but she opened the front door only an inch or two, and I couldn't see or hear my babies.

"Bob lives here now, and you'll have to speak to him. He says you can only talk to the girls in front of him. He's not here now," she mumbled through the crack. No amount of pleading changed her mind.

I pushed the door open and called for Cindy. She ran to me: I held her tight and told her how much I loved her. Mae grabbed her arm and pulled it hard, way too hard, so I let go. Then Mae pushed me to the floor and kicked me. I struggled to the door, pushed the screen door open, and fell out onto the porch. I couldn't believe what was happening.

"If you weren't so old, I would kick your ass," I yelled. I had thought Mae loved me. Now she had my children and wouldn't let me see them. But I didn't want Cindy to see me hit her grandmother—so I left the house without them. I didn't know what else to do. Again, I was out in the cold, asking God to help me.

I called my mom, but she wasn't home. Probably she wouldn't have helped me, though I had told her I was sorry about breaking into her house while she and her boyfriend were gone. She'd say, "You made your bed; now lie in it." With nowhere else to turn, I could only head back to Hollywood and Tyler. I took the next train for Los Angeles, went to the hotel, and told him I was not doing sex for money again.

A couple of days later, a friend of Tyler's told me about an opening for a cocktail waitress at a bar on Sunset Boulevard. I applied, lied about my age, and got the job. My uniform consisted of a black bodysuit with a low-cut, form-fitting top, black-mesh stockings, and black spike heels. On my behind was pinned a huge red bow. I hated the outfit because it emphasized my breasts, which the male customers stared at when I took their orders. But at least I had a real job.

At the end of the first week, I was miserable from twenty hours of walking around in high heels with the black mesh of my stockings cutting into my feet. I could hardly stand it, but I decided to go back.

The men in the bar were the same as in any other. They tried to feel me up and take me home. The tips were not generous, and the money I'd managed to save was running out. After a few hours on my second night, it was just too easy to tell myself, "I might as well give in and make some dough."

An older man sitting at the bar listened to my sad story . . .

"If I took you home, how much money would you need?"

"Only twenty-five dollars."

"When do you get off work?"

"In a couple of hours."

In two hours, he was back. I took him to my motel room, in a few minutes gave him what he wanted, and had what I needed. I cried myself to sleep.

When I returned to work the next afternoon, the owner of the bar confronted me. He had found out I was not twenty-one. I was not old enough to serve liquor and would have to leave. He refused to pay me even the little I had earned. I walked out of the bar and into the street, soon cursing at every man driving by in a fancy car. I was beginning to hate men.

I didn't understand what I had done wrong, what I had done to deserve being out on the street again. All I wanted was to be loved and to love my daughters. Whatever it was, I wasn't going to give up trying for what I wanted. I walked to a pay phone and called Tyler, who came to pick me up. On the way to my motel, I complained about how unfairly I'd been treated by the bar owner and about how much I hated serving cocktails.

"No problem, honey. I've got some guys you can see," he said. I didn't realize it, but he was leading me, little by little, into being his moneymaker—*teaching* me to be his moneymaker!

The next day, I dressed in one of a couple of new outfits I had been able to buy and went to look for another job. I stuck Mom's dinner dress into the bag in case I needed to look older. My search was a failure, and I returned to my room—the manager wouldn't let me in unless I paid the week's rent! I didn't have it, so again I was on the street, almost penniless, with the clothes on my back plus the dress in my bag.

Tyler was home when I called him to rescue me again. "Honey, I'm going to Las Vegas," he said. "Why don't you come along?"

"Come and get me!"

When Tyler pulled up, I jumped in, throwing my bag in the back seat.

"Where's the rest of your stuff?"

"Oh, I left it with one of the girls at the bar. She's not home now, so I guess I'll have to leave it." I didn't want Tyler to know I'd been locked out of the motel for not paying the rent. That would be admitting I was unable to manage my money. I sensed, even at that point, that it could give him some kind of control.

Tyler pulled onto the freeway, and I was on my way to Las Vegas!

15

Tyler pulled onto the Las Vegas strip about 9 P.M. I'm not sure of the day, but it was sometime in September 1960. I'll never forget the thousands of flashing, whirling, spinning lights, fronting the casinos. He drove up to the Sahara Hotel and registered as I waited in the car. We brought up our bags, showered together, crawled into bed, and slept.

An hour and a half later, I woke up with Tyler on top of me, making love. I was still fuzzy from the liquor we consumed on the way to Vegas. He went at it and finished fast. He kissed me lightly on the cheek and was off to shower again, with me right behind. Tyler was in a hurry: "Come on, baby! Hurry up and get something on. I want to show you off!"

Excited, I applied a little makeup and slipped into my mom's dress. I thought this town would be my salvation. Tyler took me to a restaurant at the Sahara for dinner (I hadn't eaten for a day), and I ate like a horse! Then he gave me twenty dollars and showed me how to play blackjack. I sat at a blackjack table and nobody asked for my ID. I won sixty dollars, and after a few drinks we returned to the room to sleep.

The next morning, before we left the room, Tyler said, "Here." He handed me a pill. "Take this upper. It will keep you awake and keep you skinny." I did take it, and that was the start of my pill-popping years.

We went to the cocktail lounge at the Stardust. Before long, Tyler said, "See that old man in a suit at the end of the bar? I want you to go over there and start talking to him."

"Oh, no! I can't do that." As far as I was concerned, I was with Tyler. I didn't want to meet any more men to get money.

"Oh, yes, you can," Tyler said. "As beautiful as you are, you can do anything you want."

"But I don't want to!"

"Well, we're short of money," he said, irritated, motioning me out of the lounge.

"Let's just go back to the blackjack tables," I suggested. "With my luck, we can win as much as we need."

"How much money do you have?"

I counted the bills in my purse and held up forty-two dollars.

"Look," he said. "I have ten dollars. The room tonight will cost twenty-five and dinner another ten, not to mention gambling. So you see, we need money! Just go into the lounge and sit at a table and smile at every man you see. Pretty soon, one of them will buy you a drink. When he does, ask him if he wants to have some fun with you. Go!" He pushed me towards the lounge. "Go now! You can do it. Come on. At least try!"

"Okay, okay!" I walked into the lounge and sat at an empty table; Tyler sat at the bar and watched. Whenever a man looked at me, I smiled, and minutes later, a well-dressed, older man, wearing diamond rings and expensive shoes, asked whether he could sit down and buy me a drink. We talked about the casinos, and eventually I talked about my children.

"Oh, I can help you out if you need some money."

"Yes, I do. I need money desperately."

He gave me a key: "Meet me in my room." Then he left.

I looked back at Tyler. He nodded and said, "Good job. Now go. Go do it. I'll be right here waiting for you."

I walked slowly from the lounge to the man's room. I was scared, but the pills and drinks had loosened me, and I decided to make the best of it. I turned the key in the door and walked into the room. The man was sitting at the table. He had drinks brought up, and we sat and talked about my kids and how I'd gotten into this business and ended up in Vegas. He was shocked because I was so young.

"Well, I can give you fifty dollars if that will help."

"Oh, my God, that would help a lot. "

So he handed me fifty dollars, and I took off my dress, leaving on my panties and garter belt. I lay down beside him on the bed and gave him a blow job. I left immediately to go back downstairs to show Tyler the quick money.

"See, I told you, you could do it," he said. "You were upstairs twenty minutes, and you made fifty bucks. See, you've got it in you, honey. You're beautiful, and men dream of having a woman like you."

After treating me to another big meal and a night of making love, the next morning Tyler suggested, "Why don't you go out and buy yourself a beautiful dress and go out again tonight?"

"Why do I have to do that again? I just want to be with you. I hate that job. I want a real job at a casino, with a steady paycheck."

"Well, because you're the best," he laughed. "You don't want to stop now! You're just getting the hang of it! Do it for your girls." Tyler pushed me out of our room towards the car.

We went to a nearby department store, and I bought a dress of flowing blue chiffon, long-sleeved, with a plunging neckline. It was stunning. Tyler dropped me at the Sands and returned to the hotel.

One of the men I had been with hadn't wanted to wear a rubber, and I was uncomfortable having no protection. No way did I want another pregnancy and I didn't really know what was available, so I scheduled a doctor's appointment. He gave me a prescription for a diaphragm that I could insert before having intercourse and remove to wash before its next use. He said it was 99 percent foolproof. I thought that was the best thing invented for women. Now all I had to worry about was disease.

In the Regency Lounge, a pleasant man in his fifties wearing a black toupee approached me. He bought me a drink and, after talking about gambling, escorted me to his room. In just a few minutes, I had collected a hundred-dollar bill.

I took a cab back to the Sahara to show Tyler. On the way, I thought about this being a way to make fast money and how I could save a bundle in no time and get my daughters back. The cab dropped me off, and again I ran to show Tyler what I'd earned.

"Honey, I'm so proud of you!" he said, kissing me. "But I have to go to work tomorrow. I want you to stay in Las Vegas and keep on doing what you've been doing so well."

"No! I want to go with you. Don't leave me here." I started to cry.

Holding me, he said, "I love you. We'll be together soon."

I believed him and stayed.

On Sunday morning we checked out of the Sahara and found a "pay by the week" room at the Colonial Inn, a block from the Sands. The small room was clean and comfortable enough for me. I hung up my two evening dresses and some other clothes I'd bought earlier in the week and made myself at home. Tyler returned to Los Angeles.

I was lonely at first, but the thought of making such good money cheered me. I went out every night, soon learning that the men I hustled were called "tricks" or "johns." And they had big money to throw around.

I spent the next two months on my own, making and saving money. Usually I went into a lounge, sat at a table, and introduced myself to the waiter. As time passed I met the casino (or pit) bosses and the hotel owners, who could introduce me to the high rollers. I always dressed to kill and I tipped well, so the bosses and owners liked me in their establishments. In time they catered to me as if I were a movie star, and I always treated them with respect. They trusted me, and I trusted them not to introduce me to anyone dangerous or not in good standing.

The pit bosses at the hotels called me "Baby Jane." To them I was a sweet Kewpie doll with blond hair, a round face with full lips, and a good set of knockers. I was a down-to-earth, fun-loving gal with a party personality. Most of my tricks were show-business personalities or millionaires good for the hotel business. I sold my skills as a call girl to a lot of wealthy, male cheaters who left their wives at home and came to Las Vegas willing to pay to have fun.

Every day I paid to have my hair and nails done. I got to know everyone in the shops, and I bought expensive evening clothes and accessories to show off in the clubs. At night, I sauntered into the Sands or another hotel, working to make every head turn. Men drew close to touch or stare at my clothes, face and, body, to inhale my expensive perfume. The women there enjoyed my taste in clothes and jewelry.

Many casino girls were notorious for copping their johns' chips and stashing them in a secret pocket in their mink stoles. I didn't do that, and that's why the casino bosses trusted me. They knew I kept my mouth shut about the personal lives and fantasies lived out in their hotel rooms.

Turning tricks was never fun; it was work, and I wouldn't have been there if I hadn't needed money. Once you're in, though—once you start making that much, it's hard to get out. I might have tried a job as a showgirl, but my lifestyle soon cost too much to live on a showgirl's paycheck.

Occasionally, Tyler called from Los Angeles, asking me to send him two or three hundred dollars. I wired it to him immediately. He never said what it was for, but I assumed he needed it for his business or that he was just short of cash. This put a dent in my savings, but I often made up for it by picking up an extra trick or two during the week. My average was two or three tricks per day.

During my first month in Las Vegas, I missed my period. Several months later, I missed it again. My diaphragm had failed, and I was in trouble. I couldn't have a baby; I didn't want a baby: God only knew who the father might be! The most important thing was to get my kids back; I couldn't show up pregnant in divorce court. I was desperate.

Abortions then were illegal in the United States, and no legitimate doctor or hospital performed them. A "back alley" procedure was the only choice, but finding a doctor was difficult. You had to have the right connections. And the risks were high; many women died because of unsanitary conditions or complications.

I called Tyler as soon as I was sure I was pregnant, and he returned to Las Vegas the next weekend. "The only way you can get an abortion is to go to Mexico," he said. "There are doctors in Mexicali who can fix you up. We can get you down there in a day or two, and you'll be back before you know it, good as new."

I was relieved when Tyler said he would take care of it for me, but I was terrified about what might happen in a strange country with an unknown physician, if there even would be one. I had never been to Mexico, much less gone there for an abortion. Tyler made some arrangements, and three days later I was on a plane to Mexicali. Judy, a friend I had met at the Sahara, went with me, as she had been there herself a year or so before.

Once the plane landed, we found ourselves in one of the thickest infestations of crickets in the history of Mexico. Billions of crickets were everywhere—on the runway and literally covering the roads into town. Smashed crickets covered the sidewalks, crickets got in our hair, and crickets crawled up our legs. Everywhere, there were crickets! This, combined with the heat and humidity, made me more miserable than I already was.

Somehow, we found our way to the motel that Tyler had arranged for us. It was a sleaze hole! The cover on the one single bed was stained, the bathroom fixtures were rusty and coated with deposits, and the room was dingy and dark. One small table and a chair were the only pieces of furniture other than the bed. A single light bulb hung from the ceiling, dangling at the end of an electric cord. There was no telephone or radio. After we were in the room for an hour, the manager, a disagreeable old woman, knocked on the door and threw an armload of blankets and sheets at me. They were as grimy as the room.

That night, Judy slept on top of the bedcover, and I slept sitting in the chair. Neither of us changed clothes.

My appointment was for the next morning. After getting no sleep, I felt even more scared, guilty, and miserable. I wasn't prepared for the next step, but Judy talked me into getting ready for the abortionist. His office was only a few blocks from the motel, so we walked to the address Tyler had written on a slip of paper before I left Las Vegas. The crickets swarmed again. We had to watch our feet to keep from slipping on them.

I gasped when we arrived at an old, two-story, clapboard building; it hadn't seen a coat of paint in twenty years, and it looked as if it would fall down any moment. A crudely lettered sign on the side read, "Dr. Jaramillo." An arrow pointed to the second floor, and a row of rickety stairs there led to the doctor's office. Climbing the first two stairs, I felt them move beneath my feet. I could smell mold and wood rotten from the Mexican heat.

"I can't do this," I said. "This is going to kill me." I thought I would die if I went through this procedure with this doctor in this place. Something told me that if I didn't get out of there, I wouldn't go back to the United States alive. In an hour, we were back at the airport. Judy and I drank coffee and talked until the next plane left for Las Vegas.

I called Tyler to talk about the horrible place he had sent me. I was upset, and he seemed unsympathetic. Still, after a few minutes, he convinced me that I still needed him to help solve my problem.

"The only thing you can do now is to force an abortion yourself."

"Force it myself? Are you crazy?"

"It's too bad you chickened out on your chance in Mexico because the only other way is quite a bit harder on you. You'll have to stick a coat hanger or a tube up into your womb. It could take a few hours for you to get rid of the fetus."

"Oh, my god. No way am I going to do that. I'd rather die than do that!" I couldn't believe what he was saying. I had thought he would help me through this terrible time and now he didn't even seem to care about me. But I had no choice—I had to trust him. I dreaded the idea of aborting the baby; I knew it was wrong. But I was going forward under Tyler's direction.

"I have a friend who knows the ropes, and I'll call her when you're ready to go through with it," Tyler said. "Things will be okay, honey. I'll stay with you when you decide to do it."

"Okay, Tyler. I'll call you when I'm ready."

"I'll get the stuff you need and bring it with me this weekend."

It took at least three days for me to decide to do it. In the meantime, I took more diet pills, drank cocktails, and turned tricks to make more money in case something went wrong. It made me feel better to know I was wanted by the men in the casinos, that I could make money even while I was pregnant. I didn't tell any trick about my condition or show any sign of it.

With my courage up and the money stashed, I told Tyler I was ready. He went to a drug store Saturday morning and came back with a three-foot length of clear, plastic, flexible NG tubing, about as wide as a pen. He also had a jar of Vaseline. Then he called his friend Corinne, whom I didn't know, and asked her to help. When Corinne arrived at the motel, we were ready to begin. I took four drinks of whiskey straight, to relax, and Tyler gave me sleeping pills. He told me to lie on the bed, put my legs up, and bend my knees. He coated the end of the tube with Vaseline.

"Now, Corinne will stick the tube straight in," he told me. "When it stops, it hits a wall. Then push the tube in harder, and it'll go through."

She inserted the tube into my vagina, and I could feel it going up inside me, inch by inch. It hit the wall, and she pushed harder and harder, but the tube wouldn't go through. It was painful, and the more she worked it, the more it hurt. Corinne tried to help me by moving it back and forth and up and down, but something seemed to be in the way.

"Come on, honey! You're not trying hard enough," Tyler scolded.

"It's as far in as it will go," I said. "This isn't going to work, Tyler. Can't we do something else? . . . I should just keep the poor little baby. But I can't do that or I'll never get my girls back!" I was crying aloud.

"I have one more idea," he said.

Tyler went to the closet and took a wire hanger from the rack. After pulling it apart, he straightened it and clipped off the twisted end with a pair of pliers. He took his lighter from his pocket and scorched the end of the wire, then wiped it off with a rag he had soaked with rubbing alcohol. He pushed the hanger through the tube still inside me, forcing it to the end, then clipped it to about two feet. This time Tyler pushed. Corinne watched from the end of the bed. I could see her cringe.

"Now relax, honey. This will only hurt a minute," Tyler said. Then he shoved so hard I felt I was being stabbed. A wave of terrible pain rolled over me. I screamed as the hanger pierced deep inside. I was sweating, trembling, trying not to throw up. I wanted to jump off the bed.

"Hold her down, Corinne," Tyler barked. "Help me keep this thing in her."

Corinne held both my legs down on the bed, but she didn't touch the tube, and she couldn't look at me. She turned her head towards the window and shut her eyes.

After one more push, Tyler decided the hanger and tube had gone far enough. With one hand pressed against my vagina, he held the tube between two fingers so that it wouldn't slip out, and with the other he pulled out the hanger. The tube was now partly buried inside of me, the other part hanging on the bed. I was in agony. I prayed to God to forgive me. I cried hard, crazy with pain. Finally I looked between my legs to see the tube that was hurting me so much.

"Now I want you to stay here until I say you can get up," Tyler told me. "It'll take about twelve hours. The air going up the tube will break the sack that holds the baby. You'll bleed a little, but it's nothing to get worried about. When it turns bright red, we'll know it's time to pull out the tube."

Tyler put four sleeping pills into my hand. I swallowed them with another swig of whiskey.

"I'm going to take Corinne home. Then I'm going out for awhile," Tyler said. "Now, don't you move. Those pills will make you sleep, and before you know it I'll be home, and it'll all be over."

"Tyler," I mumbled, already feeling the pills, "How do you know so much about all this?"

"Experience, honey, experience," he said, winking at me. He put on his coat, picked up the car keys, and opened the motel room door.

Corinne turned as she walked out behind him. "Good luck, sweetie," she said. "You'll be all right. Trust Tyler. You're in good hands."

I slept for four hours. My full bladder woke me, but I couldn't get up and ruin the procedure. Instead, I closed my legs tight and stared at the ceiling, thinking about my daughters. I thought too about what was happening to the baby inside. I cried for it and for myself.

Four hours later, I looked at the tube again. I had avoided it before, but now I could feel something warm coming from inside, and I had to know what was happening. I almost screamed—the towels Tyler had put beneath me were covered with blood! The blood, coming from my vagina, was bright red. When I recovered from the sight, I decided it must be time to take out the tube. I gently pulled it from my vagina, feeling its slide all the way from the inside of my womb. It came out easily, and I tossed it into the wastebasket beside the bed. I lay there for a few more seconds. All I could think of was how I wanted to take a shower, to wash away all the blood, to come clean.

When I rose up from the bed, I saw more blood coming from between my legs. It seemed to be pouring from me! I thought I was bleeding to death, panicked, and picked up the phone to call the front desk.

"Oh my God, I'm bleeding to death. Call an ambulance. Please help me! Please help me!" I pleaded. "I'm bleeding, and it won't stop! I'm in Room 17. Please hurry! I need help!"

In seconds, the manager was at the door with a passkey. When he saw the blood and how frightened I was, he called the operator, who connected him to an ambulance service. In minutes, an ambulance, sirens screaming, was carrying me to the hospital.

I was admitted to the emergency room of Sunrise Hospital. A doctor asked me questions as two nurses tried to stop the bleeding.

"It looks to me like you're having a miscarriage, Mrs. Harvey," he concluded. I didn't tell him that Tyler had caused it. "We'll see what we can do to stop it, but you're going to have to lie very still and do what the nurses tell you, or we may lose the baby."

I was taken to a room, and a nurse stuck an IV tube into a vein near my wrist.

"This will stop what's happening to you," she told me. "You just get some rest, and we'll be back to check on you in an hour or so."

For two days, as the medicine tried to work a miracle, I did everything I could to stop it, tightening the muscles in my abdomen and bearing down with as much force as I could to push the fetus from my body. Again and again, hour after hour, I strained and pushed, grunted, and sweated. When a nurse came in to check on me, I stopped, but during the rest of the time I was awake I worked to start the bleeding again, to finish what Tyler had started. It didn't work.

Finally, in desperation, on April 15, 1961, I took a straw from the glass of ice water on my table. I stuck it as far up my vagina as I could, until I could feel it touch something. I pushed and prodded with the straw until I felt a pain building inside my abdomen. I knew it was a labor pain. I pulled the straw out and began pushing again.

In half an hour, it was done. I felt something slide from inside of me, and when I looked between my legs, I saw the fetus, a tiny thing, about the size of a bird. Still curled up inside its clear little sack, it would have fit into the smallest part of my hand. I could see its little arms and legs. I called for the nurse. I had no idea that it would look like a real baby in just two months!

While the nurse cleaned me up, I thought about the baby. I wanted to die. I didn't feel evil but pitiful and full of pity, for both the baby and me. I felt I had done the worst possible thing a woman can do— to kill a child I was carrying. No amount of cheer or support from the nurse could make me feel good. I was depressed, alone.

Later, I was taken to surgery for a D & C, to clean out all the blood and tissue remaining from the pregnancy. I didn't tell the doctors or the nurses that I had not miscarried but aborted the baby on my own. I was twenty years old, and I was scared for my life.

During the three days I was in the hospital, Tyler never called or visited me. In fact, no one did. At that point I knew so few people in Las Vegas that I really didn't have any friends. Tyler was the only one.

The day I got out, I took a taxi to the motel. Tyler was sitting on the bed, holding a drink and watching television. "Hi, honey. Are you all right?" he asked with a kiss.

"Do I look all right? Do you know where I've been, what I've been through? . . . I'm tired. I'm sick. I hurt. And I'm bloated like a blimp! And you never, not once, came to see me in the hospital. Did you even know where I was?"

"Oh, sure, the manager told me," Tyler replied nonchalantly. "But you know honey, I couldn't come."

"Why?"

"Don't you see? They might think it was my kid. They would have thought I was the father to that poor little kid, and they would have asked me a bunch of questions."

"You were just afraid you'd have to pay the bill!" I snorted. "Don't you worry, Tyler, you're not responsible for it or for me. I hate what you did."

Tyler handed me a cocktail, and I calmed down as I drank. He pulled me onto the bed with him and tried to cuddle up, nuzzling my ear and cheek with his day-old stubble. As he nicey-niced, I began to think about how I was just a sucker. After eight months, I was beginning to figure out that Tyler was just using me to make money. He didn't love me; he was playing me. He knew all along I would do anything for him so long as I thought I needed him.

Our relationship was a game. He didn't care about me or about my kids. He didn't care about the baby he helped me to kill so that I could keep my children. He knew all along I was in a state of confusion about my life. Suddenly I saw that Tyler was simply watching out for Tyler—the only thing I was important to him was for the money I brought in.

"So, honey, when are you gonna go back out on the strip?" he whispered.

I flipped, jumping up to throw a pillow at him: "You are the filthiest, low-life man I have ever known! . . . You don't care about me! You don't care about anyone else except yourself. You self-centered son-of-a-bitch! I want you out of my life. I don't ever want to see you again!"

"Oh honey, you don't mean that." He took my hand and tried to pull me close.

Tears streamed down my face as I pushed him away. "Just leave me alone! Just get out of here." I shouted.

I don't think Tyler expected to hear that from me. But "poor little Janie" meant business, and Tyler didn't argue. He reached for his coat and pulled a big bag of diet pills from the pocket.

"Here, take these diet pills. You said you felt bloated. They'll make you feel a hell of a lot better."

"Get out!"

Tyler picked up his coat, grabbed his bag from beneath the bed, and walked out. "You bitch!" He slammed the door behind him.

16

I called Carol in Anaheim and told her what I'd done.

"Oh Jane, you're so young and foolish and scared of losing your daughters, you didn't think straight," she said. "I'm sure God has forgiven you. Please try to understand you are forgiven. God loves you, and so do I."

"Thanks Carol. I needed you to be my friend and say it was okay." I cried myself to sleep, thinking about how sad it was to lose my little boy, how hard my life was. I knew I had gotten myself in deep, but the next morning I decided to put a smile on my face, move forward, try to take better care of myself.

That wasn't the end of it, of course, and I'm almost afraid to tell the rest—the reader may judge me and stop reading, may have stopped reading already. But in hopes my story will help some other woman, I continue.

Four days later, Tyler called me at my apartment to say he was sorry. He loved me and missed me and wanted me to know how hurt he was that I didn't want to see him. I said I missed him too. I was sorry for getting so crazy, but I was so sick after the abortion I couldn't think straight. I put the blame on him, though I was the one desperate to do it.

Then he said, "Honey, isn't the hearing for your kids coming up?"

"Yes. In a few weeks."

"Can I come and take you there?"

"Yes, I would like that, Tyler. It would be wonderful to have your support. I know I'm going to be a nervous wreck."

So Tyler came to stay with me, and for the next two weeks we had a wonderful time. I was still sore, and he left me alone in the bed to heal. After a few days we searched for a larger apartment, one big enough for the girls and me. We moved my belongings to the new place, and then we went shopping. I had a ball buying cute little dolls and teddy bears to put around my daughters' new twin beds. I pictured them sleeping there and living with me in the apartment. I thought everything would be perfect because I'd worked hard to prove I could care for them. No one knew or cared where I got the hundred-dollar bills to pay for everything.

The day before the divorce/custody hearing (in June 1961), Tyler drove me in the red Thunderbird I'd purchased (I got my driver's license in Seattle when I was seventeen) to the Beverly Hills Hotel. There I got us a room for the next few days. The hearing was scheduled for the next morning in Santa Ana. I wanted more than anything to get custody of Cindy and Roberta. I had proof of a furnished apartment for them, and I was sure the decision would go my way—I was their mother.

Still, the night before the hearing I couldn't think straight. I rambled on to Tyler about my marriage and about how Bob's mother had pushed me down and kicked me in front of the girls. Tyler was patient and said he'd do anything to help me. In my mind, I saw Tyler getting a job and me quitting the profession. We would get a house, maybe with a white picket fence, and we would raise my daughters. Everything would be wonderful. Little did I suspect that that was the farthest thing from his mind. He knew he had a goldmine, and he was going to bleed it dry.

That night, I took some downers to get some sleep, and in the morning I took diet pills to be wide awake at the hearing. On the way to Santa Ana, I felt sick to my stomach, like I was going to throw up. I asked Tyler to pull the car to the side of the road and opened the door to vomit, but I just had the dry heaves.

When we got to the courthouse, I had him drop me off in the front and sent him on to have breakfast. I didn't want anyone to see me with him, no questions about who he was or how he was connected. These were my children, and I was going to get them back myself. It was my responsibility.

Earlier I had arranged to meet my attorney, the one I had met and hired at the Disneyland Hotel. Outside the courtroom, I paid him twelve hundred dollars to take care of my divorce, before we went in to face the judge. As we walked into the courtroom, he said, "I hate to tell you this, but your kids are here in the courtroom."

"No! They can't be here and see this. You can't subject those little girls to this. What in the hell's wrong with that family that they would bring those kids into the courtroom? Anyone with any sense knows better than to bring children to a divorce hearing!" I wanted to see Cindy and Roberta, but I didn't want them to witness the legal proceedings.

"Just calm yourself down," he said. "When we walk into the room, don't run over to them and grab them. Don't make a scene."

We went through the swinging doors of the courtroom, and I saw Cindy and Roberta sitting to the right, behind Bob and his attorney. Bob's sister and his mother, Mae, were sitting with the girls, one on each side. Cindy and Roberta jumped up and ran over, shouting, "Mommy, Mommy, Mommy!" They threw their arms around me.

I knelt to hug and kiss them. After a minute, I told them to go sit down, that I had to sit with the man in the suit on the other side of the aisle. I would talk with them later.

I sat down next to my attorney, leaned over, and whispered, gritting my teeth, "Get my children out of this courtroom now! And I mean now. Or I'm going to throw the biggest fit this court has ever seen." He just looked at me, but I think he believed I would do it.

The judge entered, and everyone stood up. When he was seated, my attorney remained standing.

"My client wishes to have her children taken out of this court hearing. She does not want them subjected to this procedure," the attorney said, directly to the judge.

Immediately the judge granted the request, agreeing that children had no place at such a proceeding. A marshal escorted the girls to the judge's chambers. Cindy looked back over her shoulder at me, then at her father, as she was led away. She was bewildered. Roberta, at eighteen months, was too young to understand, but Cindy, three-and-a-half-years old, knew something terrible was happening.

Bob was called to the stand first. He said I was working in a nudie joint in Las Vegas and probably prostituting myself all over town. He said I was an unfit mother and that if I got the girls I wouldn't be able to take care of them. I couldn't believe he didn't defend me or say I had been a good mother. When it was my turn, I told the judge about how Mae and Bob had tricked me into giving up the kids and how Bob couldn't support the girls because he couldn't hold a steady job. I said he was a drunk and a pill popper, that was all he cared about.

I cried as I told the judge about how Bob had left me stranded with no money, food, or place to live. I pleaded with the judge to grant me custody. I told him I could do it if he'd just give me a chance. "Please give me my girls. They need their mother! I was the one with a job—at the hospital—and he cheated on me."

"Try to get ahold of yourself, Mrs. Harvey," the judge said sternly.

He didn't look sympathetic "You can step down now. I'll be back in a few minutes with my decision." He stood up, then turned to his chambers. I returned to my seat at the table and cried, now afraid the girls might not be awarded to me.

In ten minutes, the judge was back. Speaking to both Bob and me, he said, "I feel that neither of you is old enough or mature enough to take care of your two daughters. Therefore, I grant custody to Mae, the grandmother."

"But he lives with them!" I pounded on the table. "It's not fair! It's just not fair!" I fell to the floor and pounded the cold cement, crying my heart out.

"If you don't calm down, Mrs. Harvey, I'm going to hold you in contempt," the judge said, losing patience with my hysterics.

"I want my babies! I want my babies!"

The attorney grabbed my shoulders and pushed me into the chair. I instantly quieted, deciding it was easier to shut up than go to jail. Then I gave up. I sat in my chair and cried. All I could think about was what I had been doing for the past year so that I could have my babies. I had never believed I wouldn't be granted custody, and now I had lost my daughters.

I had ruined my whole life working to get Cindy and Roberta, and now it was hopeless. This was the point at which I hardened. Maybe I was too young to have kids. Maybe they were better off with Mae. I had no self-confidence, and I was drained from the ordeal, in shock.

After I quieted down, the judge continued. "I'm giving you equal visitation rights. Your divorce is granted."

"But don't I get alimony? How can I live? I need my babies!"

Cindy and Roberta were brought back into the courtroom, and I went to them to hug them and kiss them. I told them I loved them and that they would have to stay with Mae for awhile, but I would come to see them. Mae came over and took their hands. She said I could visit them whenever I wanted, but that I had to call before coming. She said she would take good care of them; despite how I felt about Mae, I knew she would.

I turned my head from the girls as I walked from the courtroom so they wouldn't see my tears. The attorney walked me to the rest room, and I washed my face and tried to calm down. I sat in the toilet stall for about twenty minutes, crying and throwing up. I didn't want to live.

Finally, I tried to reason everything out. I had visitation rights. I could fly the girls or myself back and forth when I wanted to be with them. Las Vegas had everything I needed—money (I could afford to fly), drugs, money, a place to live, money, clothes, money, furniture, money, and drugs. And more money. I would make enough to buy a place in California. I would get out soon. Of course, none of it was rational—by this time I was hooked.

I stopped turning the wheels, remembering that Tyler was in the parking lot, waiting for me, I got myself together, left the courthouse, and found him in the Thunderbird. He drove me back to Beverly Hills.

I was sick for two days, and I sobbed and sulked in the room for a week. All I could think was that I had had an abortion for no reason. I had no daughters; I should have had the baby. God forgive me for killing my baby.

Tyler stayed the whole time, trying to be supportive, holding me and assuring me that everything would be okay. Finally, he convinced me we should go back to Vegas.

The next day, before we left, I bought a bottle of scotch, and we partied all the way back to Nevada. On the way I decided I didn't want to be with Tyler any longer, and I told him I needed to be alone. I felt that if I couldn't have my daughters, I didn't want anyone. He said he understood, and he left soon after we got back to Las Vegas.

I had thought the world of Tyler, listened to him because I felt he was helping me get enough money to get custody of my girls. I hadn't realized that he'd been pimping me for months for his own benefit. I did the dirty work, gave him half the money, paid for the motel, and let him sleep with me for free. He made me feel special, and I fell for his game.

After Tyler left, I threw myself on the bed, cried myself to sleep, and stayed there, going pretty much without food for a week. I felt sad about everything but Tyler's departure.

The main thing was losing Cindy and Roberta. Mae would let me see them only when Bob was there, and because he was afraid I would take them to Vegas, I could see them only at Mae's trailer house. (She had no job—how was she going to support them?) I was afraid to return to court—the way things were going, I might lose the visitation rights I already supposedly had.

I also mourned the fetus I'd aborted; I brooded that the law had given me no right to make such a personal decision or to carry it out in a safe way. I mourned the absence of my mother's support in the courtroom. I mourned the loss of my marriage and the dreams of what my family could be. Finally, I thought about how sick I was of the men—Woody, Buck, Bob, Tyler, and, yes, the johns—using and abusing me.

I saw little choice in what to do next. I wanted to be near my daughters, but without a high-school diploma I couldn't earn a decent, legal living in Santa Ana. In Vegas I had some connections and I could make a lot more money with no one taking a cut. I'd soon have enough to get out of Vegas and buy a home in California: "Come on, high rollers—if you want me for sex, I'll go all out, and you'll pay for it, big time. Goodbye, users and abusers—you had me for awhile; now nobody gets a piece. Hello, Janie—you're on your own, and you're in control!"

I didn't consider how vulnerable I might be to the uppers and downers—to the allure of the famous name, the big money, the Vegas life—or to anyone who I thought might love me.

17

So after I got rid of Tyler, I went out on my own. One night I met a guy named Jonesy in the Casbah Lounge of the Sahara Hotel. He introduced himself, ordered me a drink, and explained his job as a pit boss in the casino. A pit boss makes sure that the dealers and stickmen at the blackjack and crap tables are alert and make sure there is no cheating. Some of the pit bosses lined up girls for their high rollers. But there were only four gals good enough, he said, to introduce to their high rollers.

When I told him I was from California, he asked, "How long have you been in Vegas?"

"Oh, about ten months."

"You're an awful pretty girl. And not built too bad. Are you going to be living here, or are you just vacationing?"

"No, I'm living here. I'm never going to leave Las Vegas." I told him I had an apartment off Desert Inn Boulevard, behind the Desert Inn Hotel.

"When you're in the casino, stop by and see me. Be sure to say hi," he said.

He seemed nice, and I said I would look him up. I knew that the people I met, especially the pit bosses, could introduce me to men with money. Jonesy eventually became one of my best contacts, and he was one of my first real friends in Las Vegas.

Late one morning, I drove to the Flamingo Lounge at the Flamingo Hotel, sat down at a table, and noticed a man in his late fifties at the bar, having a drink and carrying on with the bartender. He spotted me and yelled, "Come here, cutie! Where've you been all my life?"

I said sweetly, "Right here." I thought he was just some drunk left over from the night before.

"You'd better sit right down here and have a Bloody Mary with me," he said, pulling up another stool. "I've been coming here and appearing at this hotel for years, and I've never seen such a sweet little kitten as you. Do you live here, or are you visiting? Do you like to party?"

"Yes, I live here, and I like to party," I smiled shyly, wondering who this loud, bizarre man could be.

"My name's Joe E. Lewis," he announced. "I used to work the vaudeville circuit, but now I work here in Vegas occasionally."

I had no idea who Joe E. Lewis was, but I accepted his offer of a drink. "Who knows where this could lead?" I thought.

We talked through several Bloody Marys. He told me the history of the hotels on the strip, saying that the Flamingo, built by Benjamin "Bugsy" Siegel in 1947, was the first to put some class into Vegas: "Years ago, the city fathers wanted to keep all the clubs downtown on Fremont Street. That was way back in the 1930s and '40s. The casinos looked like nineteenth-century saloons and betting parlors."

After the Flamingo opened, Las Vegas changed. Gambling was still the big attraction, but big hotels now housed the gamblers, and big-name entertainers were brought in to draw even more. Joey (that's what I called him) said he was one of the first headliner comedians in Vegas.

He also told me about how the Mafia had owned Las Vegas before the State of Nevada clamped down on the mobsters, forcing them to put the casinos under legitimate names. Still, he said, the town was operated under the table by the Mafia boys.

As evening approached, Joey decided to go downtown to gamble, so we hopped into a cab, and in about seven minutes we were on Fremont Street at the Golden Nugget. We walked in and hit the crap tables, where we won about $500. Then we went to the blackjack tables and won $1,500.

By that time, I was loaded: "Joey, I'm getting too stoned. I have to go home."

"Oh, no, you can ride back to the Flamingo with me. You can come up and check out my etchings," he chuckled. "Besides, I want to give you a little something to take home with you."

I knew where he was leading and thought, "Oh, great! I'll make some more money." Joey had already given me the winnings from our gambling spree.

When we got back to the Flamingo, we went up to his room, and I washed up. I undressed in the bathroom and wrapped myself in a towel. When I stepped out, I saw he had taken off all but his underwear. I walked over to the bed, where Joey pulled off my towel. His eyes were as big as silver dollars, and he licked his lips, having a look-see. He lay back on the bed, and, kneeling over him, I brought his fantasy to life. Joey got excited fast, and he was off in a minute or two.

"You're something else, babe. You really know how to treat a man," Joey smiled. "Here's a little something for you." He handed me a folded bill.

"Thank you, darling," I said graciously. (I really did like the old fart.) "I'll call you tomorrow."

I caught a cab home, the next morning I called him, and we met for breakfast at the Flamingo's coffee shop. Well, *I* had breakfast, and he had a Bloody Mary. While we were sitting there, he introduced me to some of the casino pit bosses. I was sweet and gracious, and they all seemed to like me. Apparently they sensed what I was about, and each asked me to come in and see him when I was in the casino. I saw the chance to make new friends and business contacts.

After breakfast, Joey asked, "Aren't you ready for a Bloody Mary, Janie?"

"Oh, my God! How do you drink the way you do?"

"My doctors told me to stop drinking or it will kill me, but if I stop, that's what'll kill me," Joey laughed, and we were off to the lounge.

As we walked across the casino, Joey saw a friend and called to him, "Hey, Vic, what are you up to? I heard you were comin' to town. Saw your name on the billboard out there."

It was Vic Damone! "Who's that cute gal you've got with you?" Vic asked.

"This is Jane Harvey," Joey said. "Why don't you join us for a Bloody Mary?"

We sat at a table in the lounge. After one Bloody Mary, Joey announced, "I've got to catch a plane. I have to be in New York tonight. See you, kids!"

He left, and suddenly I was sitting alone with one of the most attractive singers appearing in Las Vegas. He was the tall, dark, and handsome man all women love—and unlike the men I had tricked with, he was in his mid-thirties and hunky! He had the most beautiful black hair and brown eyes!

I had heard his songs on the radio but didn't know much else about Vic Damone. I wasn't a fan, but I acted as if I were impressed to meet him. I was as charming as I could be, and we took to each other right away. He asked whether I would like to come back and see his show that night: "I'd love to."

"Just tell the maître d' to set you up front and center," Vic told me. "I'll expect to see you." He excused himself for an afternoon rehearsal.

I was excited. Here I was, just eighteen years old, with a celebrity! I decided to shop for a new outfit at the dress shop in the Flamingo, and then went to the beauty parlor. The hairdresser at the Colonial House Motel beauty salon insisted I become a blonde, and since I was beginning to meet all these new people, I thought I might as well do it then: "Blondes have more fun. Let's do it!"

He bleached my hair champagne beige and styled it in a bouffant—a stunning fashion statement. It made me look a little bit older and a whole lot more sophisticated. And the hairdresser gave me new eyelashes, so I'd look like a showgirl.

After all that was done, I went to my room at Colonial House, took a shower, put on makeup, and slid into my Mr. Blackwell evening dress. I popped a diet pill, then got into my car and drove to the Flamingo. I had a date with a celebrity, and I was going to his show in style. I drove to the Flamingo, less than a mile from my motel. I had learned by then that a lady didn't walk the streets, in Vegas or anywhere else. Besides, I had a date with a celebrity, and I was going to his show in style.

The maître d' seated me in front as Vic said he would, and I sat there enjoying his act, glorying in my first time at a show where I knew the entertainer, was even his date. And Vic was singing right to me! Like a silly girl, I blushed and put my head down. The people seated nearby looked at me and smiled, thinking, I supposed, how lucky I was to get so much attention from him.

In the lounge afterwards, we drank for awhile, then Vic said, "Why don't we get away from these people, go up to my suite?" There were crowds of tourists and gamblers, and every once in awhile someone interrupted to ask for an autograph. It was distracting.

"That sounds like fun," I agreed. "Let's go."

We had more to drink in his large, comfortable suite, and he ordered a tray of hors d'oeuvres. We talked for an hour or two, and then he kissed my neck and started running his hands over my body. He hummed a song in my ear, and I just sort of swooned and lay back to enjoy it. Soon, we were both getting excited—at least I could tell he was. Vic started taking off my clothes and then his own, and we had sex on his king-size bed. He knew how to please a woman, but he had no idea I did this for a living and I didn't bring it up. It was too much fun to ask to be paid for it.

We slept a few hours, then I nudged him to say I had to go back to my place. He asked me for my phone number, so I left it on the dresser. I put on my clothes, kissed him lightly, had my car brought up by the valet, and drove back to my apartment.

I didn't see Vic again until about four months later. Arriving at the Flamingo for my evening prowl, I looked up at the billboard, and there was "Vic Damone" surrounded by lights—I'd have to look him up. I found the courtesy phones and left a message with the desk for him to meet Jane Harvey in the cocktail lounge after his first show. Maybe he would show up; maybe he wouldn't. It would be good to see him, and possibly I could turn a trick. It was time to let him know I was in business. Even if it meant he wouldn't look at me again, I wanted him to know.

After the first show, Vic walked into the lounge. I was sitting near the front, and when he saw me, he beamed and headed in my direction: "Hi, baby! You sure look beautiful tonight. How are you doing? What's up?" Vic said.

"Oh, I was wondering how long you're going to be in town."

"I'm just here for the weekend," Vic said. "You know, I've been thinking about you lately. We sure did have a lot of fun."

As we shared a drink, Vic told me he would like to get together but that he had people in town that day and couldn't get away. He wanted to meet me the next day, see a show, and spend some time alone with me that night.

"Oh, that would be great!"

Vic said he would pick me up the next afternoon. I gave him directions to my apartment, and he left to do his next show.

I drove to the Dunes to continue my circuit. In the lounge, I spotted Major Auterburn Riddle, owner of the Dunes Hotel and a high-rolling gambler, whom I'd previously tricked. I had met him on another occasion in the casino, and we had talked a few times since. We were becoming good friends.

He joined me for drinks, and the conversation turned to the topless revues in town. He had booked the *Minsky's Follies,* starring Lou Costello, for six weeks at the Dunes. It was the first show featuring bare-breasted women, and it was an overnight sensation. It had saved his hotel, seriously in the red.

Riddle told me he also brought the French show *Casino de Paris* to Vegas. Frederic Apcar produced the Las Vegas version. That was the second bare-breasted show and another tremendous success. I think it played at least five years at the Dunes. At one time, various religious groups picketed the hotels, protesting the nudity. Then and later, the protests failed; topless shows are still a staple of Vegas entertainment.

As we talked, Riddle noticed one of his managers coming toward the lounge: "Hey, come here, Sid. I want you to meet this little doll here, Janie."

Sid Wyman joined us. A sweetheart in his late forties, he had charisma; very tall, extremely handsome, he was also a co-owner of the Dunes, Sands, Riviera, and Royal Nevada hotels. He asked, "How long have you lived here in Vegas, Janie?"

"Oh, about ten months."

Riddle excused himself, saying he had an appointment in the counting room, where the casino intake was taken for counting.

Pulling his chair closer, Sid said, "You sure are a good-looking little gal. What do you do for a living here?"

"The best I can with what I've got . . . if you know what I mean."
I winked.

"As a matter of fact, there is a friend of mine here from Chicago.
He's looking for a little plaything just like you.

"Well, let's go meet him."

We went to the blackjack table, and Sid introduced me to a Mr.
Goldbaum from Chicago. Middle-aged and somewhat stocky, he had
a sort of midwestern look.

Goldbaum handed me a stack of chips, and we gambled for hours.
I won a ton of money, and he let me keep it—all the men let me keep
any money I won. By about 5 A.M. we were getting hungry, so Goldbaum took me to the casino restaurant for a snack. Then we went to
his room to play. He wanted a trip around the world, and I gave him
the grand tour. I saw the generous gift he left for me on the dresser, so
I did a super job. He was happy with me, and I was happy with my
pocket full.

But I had to get home, get some sleep, and straighten up my new
apartment before my date with Vic. I showered and dressed in a hurry.
Goldbaum was still lying satisfied on the bed. I gave him a peck on the
cheek and slipped my phone number into his hand.

"Give me a call when you get back into town." I picked up my bag
and walked out with a wave.

At 8 P.M., Vic rang the doorbell, and I ran to let him in. We went
to dinner at the Candlelight Room in the Flamingo Hotel, where he
was appearing. It was the first gourmet restaurant opened in Las Vegas.
There was a wine steward helping Vic with his selection. The steward
pulled the cork from the bottle and poured it into a glass for Vic's
approval before serving it to me. The food was beautifully presented
and tasted fabulous. The atmosphere was elegant, the patrons sophisticated, obviously well off. Everyone seemed to be wearing diamonds;
the men all wore ties and women, long evening gowns.

We decided to skip the show and go gambling instead. We headed to the Stardust first, then jumped in a cab for the Sahara Hotel. And who did we see getting out of an elevator at the Sahara? Elvis Presley, with two gorgeous women, one on each arm. He was in such a hurry that Vic didn't get a chance to speak to him. Later that night, we saw Elvis playing the slot machines. I heard later that he had bought two Cadillacs, one for each of the girls he was with in Vegas. In each of the Caddies, he reportedly laid out a luxurious fur coat. Lucky girls!

After the Sahara, Vic took me back to the Flamingo. We were dead tired, stoned to the gills. In his room, we undressed, and he began to caress me.

"You know, Vic. I have to tell you something," I said, stopping the lovemaking for a moment. "I go to bed for money. That's how I make a good living."

He was surprised. "You've got to be kidding. A sweet little thing like you having to do that?"

"It's the only way I can make big money. I have to go to court and show I have a place for my girls to live. The only thing that's going to help me out is money."

"I understand, honey. I'm sorry this had to happen to you. You are so sweet and fun. Now come on over here!"

Vic and I lay down on the bed, and I started kissing his body and he fondled and kissed my breasts. When he was ready, I climbed on top of him. He liked to go forever, and I gave him the time he wanted. Afterwards, I got up and dressed, then picked up the gift on the dresser, and kissed him goodbye. He said he would call me the next time he was in town. As it turned out, I was never with him again, though I did see him later at one of his shows.

Back at my apartment, I lay on my bed and cried. Every day I asked God to help me get out of this life. But then I stopped crying, took a shower, swallowed some pills, and went back to the casinos.

My first stop was the Sands. I stood and talked for a few minutes to Bucky Harris, a pit boss there.

"You know who's here in the hotel?" Bucky asked.

"I didn't notice the billboard. Who is it?"

"Jerry Lewis," Bucky said as if I should have known.

"Oh, that crazy guy? He's so funny!"

"He is a fun guy. He's in his room now. Why don't you go surprise him? He starts his show tomorrow night, so he might have time for a pretty little thing like you. Let me call and see if he wants me to send you to the cottage."

Bucky went to call Jerry's room from the house phone in the pit—the place where the bosses stand to watch the transactions of money and gambling. He came back saying, "Go on over there."

I was a little nervous. I had always thought Jerry Lewis was a great entertainer, never dreaming I would meet him, much less turn a trick with him. He opened the door to his suite.

"Well come on in, sweetie. What's your name?"

"Jane Harvey."

"That's a pretty name. It fits that pretty face," Jerry said. "Sit down. Let's have a drink."

We sat there about two hours, laughing and telling jokes. I said I had always wanted to meet him, that I thought he was one of the greatest comedians in the world.

"Do you like it when I do this?" he asked. He stood, then stumbled around the room, being clumsy, feet and legs of jelly, doing his nerd routine. He cracked me up!

Jerry said I reminded him of someone he had noticed among the fans hanging around after his shows in New York. On his way from the building was a staircase where the fans gathered to get his autograph. In the crowd, over a period of time, was a girl with a beautiful face, blond hair, and green eyes. Jerry said he had never met her or talked with her but that she had always stuck in his mind.

"And you, my dear, have the same face," he said. Then he did a little song-and-dance routine: "That face, that fabulous face . . . " he chortled, at the same time he did a soft-shoe shuffle across the carpet.

By this time, we'd had a few drinks, and I noticed how soft-spoken he was, how serious he was being himself. He wasn't at all the zany, crazy guy I'd thought. He told me how much he loved his family and how hard he worked for the causes he promoted. He said he felt lonely on the road and he was glad he to meet such a sweet girl. Maybe, for a few moments, I could take some of his loneliness away.

I was thinking about how handsome he was when he was serious, how sincere. I wished he weren't attached because I felt attracted to him. I just loved him then, and I do to this day.

Jerry was almost bashful when it came to having sex, but he thoroughly enjoyed it. Still, he had a quirky way of dealing with his loyalty to his wife. He would not climax inside me, no matter what kind of sex we had.

Afterward, we had drinks, and Jerry took me to his car, a Lincoln, I think, and we went for a drive towards downtown. He showed me the recording equipment he had installed in his car. He said he practiced many of his routines using that tape recorder and played them back while he was driving. As we head back on Las Vegas Boulevard toward the Sands, we saw the sun coming up over Sunrise Mountain.

It was breathtaking! Jerry pulled the car to the side of the street, and we simply watched. Jerry said he loved the morning hours more than any part of the day. I told him I did too, but that I never got to see much of the morning because I was just going to bed. He laughed; I think he liked my sense of humor.

"I wish I had my airplane here. I love to go flying in the morning. It's the most beautiful time of day," he said.

At the Sands, Jerry drove into the circle drive in the wrong direction. He was still pretty drunk, and he was being crazy. He headed the Lincoln toward the curb and drove up onto the sidewalk near the entrance of the casino.

"I think we've landed," he screamed in his crazy, nerdy voice.

Laughing like crazy, we jumped out of the car, ran into the casino, and out the side door by the pool. We both ran around the pool twice, yelling, before heading back to the room. We fell onto the bed in stitches. We had another drink; then Jerry said we'd better eat something and sent for sandwiches. I could tell he was tired, and I said I had to leave, that I had some important things to do.

Jerry invited me to his show that night. I accepted and really enjoyed it. He saw me in the crowd, and looked right down at me. He directed some of the lines and antics in his routine straight at me. He was one of the nicest men I'd ever met.

Jerry just liked me. He liked to talk, and he felt comfortable with me. I knew that being a celebrity on the road could be hard and lonely. I think guys like Jerry thought of me as a breath of fresh air because I saw them as the persons they were, and I talked down to earth with them, as if we'd known each other for years.

One night in Los Angeles, I checked into the Beverly Hills Hotel and went to the Polo Lounge, where I met James M. Long, of Spalding Sports. He said he was senior vice president of the company that made the famous golf balls. An elderly man, he liked his chicks. He took me to lunch at the Brown Derby in Hollywood, after which we stopped at Trader Vic's for drinks. I loved that place, especially the exotic drinks.

Afterwards, I gave Long a trip around the world, then returned to Trader Vic's for another Mai Tai. I could tell a lot of wealthy guys hung around there.

A man sitting at a table next to mine looked over and smiled. I smiled back, and he walked over and introduced himself as Harry James.

"Oh, my God, the famous horn player?"

"I'm the one. You sure are a beautiful little thing." But he was kind and interested, so I didn't object. "Have you ever been to a recording studio?"

"No, but that seems like something fun to do."

"Well, I think I'm going to take you with me, but first I want to take you over to my friend's apartment, where we can get comfortable," Harry said.

"You've got it."

Afterwards, Harry told me about his ex-wife, Betty Grable. He said she was a nymphomaniac, never satisfied. He said he couldn't handle her infidelities—she had to have sex with other men to get enough—which led to their divorce. But I never did hear her side of the story.

At the recording studio, Harry took me into a room with a glass window and a lot of instrument panels. He said would be working on the other side, but I could sit in the booth and watch the recording artists. Harry was doing a song accompanied by only a few instruments and a backup singer, and I watched as they performed and re-performed it. I'd had no idea how much work went into the recording of just one song.

After the session, Harry took me for a bite to eat. I told him I was leaving for Las Vegas the next day, and that I would call him when I again returned to L.A.

We were together three more times. Harry always welcomed my phone calls and treated me well. He was at least thirty-five years older than I, but I don't think the difference crossed his mind; he was young at heart, and he just liked to have fun. It was all about money for me, but could he blow a horn! Whenever I hear the song they recorded that day, I think of Harry. Once he said I looked like Betty Grable when she was young . . .

18

When a high roller came to town, the pit bosses from the Sands, Dunes, Flamingo, Tropicana, and Desert Inn called me: "Are you available for Mr. P. right now, or are you busy?"

"No problem, I'll be there in an hour." A high-class hustler had to be ready to meet a high roller at any time of day or night. But the high rollers were willing to pay big bucks for a topnotch girl.

The casinos needed beautiful women for the high rollers because they liked to be seen going out to dinner, attending stage shows, gambling, and having drinks with someone who looked expensive. A woman hired for the evening also had to be willing to satisfy whatever private fantasies the roller might have during the period of hire.

I felt lucky to be among the 2 percent of Las Vegas women in prostitution working at this level. Hanging with the high rollers was a lot different from working the streets or in the houses. The streetwalker did it in a car—twenty-five bucks for a blow job, fifty for the whole screw. She cleaned herself with a quick wipe and a rinse of the mouth, then back to the street to do it again. The house prostitute had a place to clean up—for the price of 40 percent to the madam and whatever she gave her john.

My job, at best, was to keep the high rollers (actually, their money) in the casino of choice—but if the roller wanted to go to another casino, that was okay too. The idea was that when a high roller returned to Vegas and wanted to party, he would return to a particular hotel casino because the owner or pit boss could hook him up with me. If he wanted more girls, or more for his friends, I could supply that too.

High rollers liked me because I knew how to please a man in many ways, because I could walk and talk the gambling game, and because I was trustworthy. Every day, I had my hair and nails done, and I always wore a beautiful dress, to make each date a special occasion. I could put on my face as quick as lightning, put on a bra, garter belt, hose, and a dress in minutes.

I carried myself well, entering a casino with shoulders back, head high, eyes forward. I knew how to get people to look at me, and I knew just what the men wanted to see. When I was with a money-man, I laughed and screamed at the crap tables to get the hundred-dollar chips flowing like water. Out on my own, I could always spot the high roller who wanted to have fun with a doll on his arm.

In the 1960s, the casinos never allowed girls off the streets in to hustle. If they tried, the vice cops escorted them out or arrested them for loitering. Only a few hustlers were accepted—actually invited: Annette, Audrey, Patsy Lee, Laurie, and me. We were the queen bees of Vegas—elegant, charming, witty, seemingly carefree, beautiful, and fun. We didn't steal, cheat, complain, or take stories of sex out of the bedroom.

During my first year alone in Las Vegas, I hustled seven days a week, making sure the pit bosses and casino owners knew me. They heard I was the top B-Jin—the guys said I was the best in town.

Harry Goodheart, a Sands boss in his early fifties, was one of my good connections. I first met him one afternoon in the Regency Lounge. He was friendly and always listened to my stories, sometimes offering advice and support. He never judged me, and I looked forward to seeing him every time I went into the Sands.

I became friends with Annette, one of the elite call girls, through my friend Jonesy, pit boss at the Sahara. I was on the hunt, sitting in the lounge at a table near the bar when Jonesy brought Annette to meet me.

"I thought you might have things to talk about," Jonesy said, turning to leave after accomplishing his good deed for the day.

Annette was not what I would call beautiful, but she was an attractive brunette, slender but shapely. Five or six years older than I, she was outgoing and down to earth, and we got along right away. After a few minutes of small talk, Annette asked, "Would you like to meet someone, a high-paying guy who's coming to town tomorrow?"

"Honey, I'd like to meet anyone who pays big bucks." Then I told her about my daughters and how I was trying to save money to bring them to Vegas for a visit.

"Well, I think you'd like him, and I know he'd like you. I'm sure he could help you, too."

"What's his name?" I asked, my curiosity growing.

"Oh, Frank Sinatra," she said casually.

"Oh . . . my . . . God! *The* Frank Sinatra? You're kidding!"

"No, I'm not kidding. Listen. Frank's coming to town tomorrow, and I want you to meet him. He's staying at the Sands while he's performing, and we can meet there tomorrow afternoon when he gets in. They're making a movie called *Ocean's Eleven*."

"Wow, that's exciting! Okay, I'll try it, but I don't know if I can pull if off." The "what-ifs" struck—the thought of being with such a big name made my stomach drop to my feet. I didn't want to do something stupid. I knew I'd have to look especially good for a guy like Frank to like me.

"Don't worry, honey. He'll love you. Frank likes girls who are young, natural, and beautiful. Just be yourself. You'll do just fine, and I'll be right there to help you."

For the next twenty-four hours, I was a nervous wreck. I could hardly sleep, and it wasn't diet pills keeping me awake. In my mind I dressed and undressed myself a hundred times, trying on everything in my closet. I got up in the middle of the night and fussed with my hair, trying different styles—more sophisticated, older, younger, classier. I didn't know what impression to make.

The next morning, I decided that nothing in my wardrobe was acceptable—I needed something new. And I decided to let my hairdresser at the Colonial House choose a "do" for me. He'd know how a girl should look when she met a star.

I didn't trick anyone that day but devoted the whole morning and afternoon to getting ready for my introduction to Frank Sinatra. I searched frantically through the dress shops, finally settling on a tight, double-knit dress with a plunging neckline and spaghetti straps. The dress was lemon yellow at the top, gradually changing to a darker yellow toward the hem. It was covered with yellow sequins, sparkling wherever the light hit them. It had a sequined jacket that I could remove if I wanted to reveal what was hidden beneath. I found a pair of white six-inch heels and had them dyed to match.

After shopping, I headed to my hairdresser, Jim, at the Colonial House. He was almost as excited as I to hear I was going to meet Sinatra that evening.

"Listen, dear. We'll make you look like a princess. I hear Frank likes princesses."

"You can forget the tiara," I laughed.

He did his magic. When I walked out of that salon, I had hair a foot high. He had attached a hairpiece of cascading ringlets to the top of my head. In back, more ringlets fell almost to the middle of my shoulders. The sides swept up and back, forming a nest for all the curls. I probably looked like a walking waterfall, but I thought it was perfect.

With only a couple of hours before meeting Annette and Frank at the Sands, I went to my apartment and took a quick bubble bath. I wanted to smell, feel, and taste sweet that night! I took more time than usual, putting on my eyelashes and getting into the dress. I was "a thousand points of light," even in the dim apartment. I was ready! I popped two diet pills, downed them with a glass of water, and headed out.

My hands were sweating and shaking as I walked through the entrance to the Sands casino. Scared to death, I needed a drink to calm me down. I headed straight for the Regency Lounge, where I was to meet Annette. Finding an open space at the bar, I ordered a cocktail. To the right, I could see a crowd gathering around a roped-off area in the lounge. There was a lot of noise and laughing. I spotted Annette at about the same time she spotted me. She motioned for me to join her. I couldn't! Not yet. She must have seen my panic because she pushed her way through the crowd and joined me at the bar.

"Let's go to the ladies' room, and I'll fix your makeup," she said.

I went, happy to stall the inevitable.

When I told her how nervous I was, Annette reassured me. "Just relax, Janie. There are just a few of Frank's friends over there. They won't bite you. Frank's at the tables. He'll be back in a few minutes."

That didn't help much, but at least I was with someone who understood how I felt. She looked me over, making sure my hair and makeup were perfect; then we walked back into the lounge, through the crowd, and into the roped-off area. There, seated at a table, were Sammy Davis Jr. and Dean Martin. Annette introduced me as we joined them.

"Would you like a drink?" Dean asked.

"Yes," I smiled, thinking to myself, " Boy, do I!" Pausing a moment, I replied, "I'd like scotch and water."

The waiter delivered the drinks in a hurry, and I sipped away as I listened to Sammy and Dean's silly jokes. I was quiet, shy. I watched and smiled and laughed when everyone else did, but I didn't have much to say. I had never been that close to two superstars, and it was a bit intimidating.

After a few minutes, Frank walked in and sat down next to me. He was in his mid-forties at the time, still dashing. Although I wasn't usually physically attracted to older men, I was drawn to him from the start.

"Who's this cute little doll?" Frank asked Annette.

"Frank, this is Jane Harvey."

I smiled and said, "Hello." That's the only word I could muster. I felt faint and giddy, just like some star-struck teenager.

Frank kept looking at me out of the corner of his eye. When I looked at him, he winked and flirted with me. "You are such a pretty girl. Where are you from?"

"Fullerton, California. I'm just a hometown girl."

"Well, I'll bet your hometown misses you," he said, laughing.

Frank and I talked quietly for a few minutes while Annette, Sammy, and Dean carried on. I told him I once lived in Hawaii and he said he'd been there too and knew how nice the people there were. After awhile I began to feel more comfortable . . . these men were just ordinary people except that they happened to be famous and wealthy. I believed Frank and the boys would take good care of me and pay me well. How could I possibly go wrong being around them? And there would be other celebrities because of the shooting of *Ocean's Eleven*. The Rat Pack worked on that during the day and performed at the Sands at night.

I began to relax. The party girl was back.

Soon Frank excused himself to get ready for his first show. I think he did two shows a night, the second starting at midnight. "I'll see you at the late show tonight, then?" he asked.

"Oh, yes, I'll be there, if you want me to come!"

"You be there!" Frank winked as he walked from the table. I saw him give Annette a thumbs-up. Apparently I had passed Frank's first inspection.

After more drinks in the lounge, Annette, Sammy, Dean, and I walked to the entrance of the Copa showroom to be seated front and center. Once again, I was within a few feet of a performer singing directly to me. The room was full, and I could feel the excitement of people about to see Sinatra in person, performing the songs they loved to hear.

When Frank hit the stage, the room exploded. People stood and applauded, and he graciously waited for them to be seated before he began. He was at the peak of his career and his voice, I thought, had never been better. The adoring crowd spurred him on, and he didn't disappoint. He was wonderful!

Through Frank's performance, when he was near our table, he gazed into my eyes as he sang, the way he looked at any woman he wanted. That was one of his charms, I soon learned. It was intoxicating for me, and I could imagine how other women felt when each of them was the object of his desire, of his sexy blue eyes.

Frank had asked me to meet him backstage after the show. We went up to his room, where I spent the rest of the night cuddled in his arms. In the morning I went back to my apartment, Frank to the sauna to sweat off the liquor he devoured the night before.

Two days later, I joined Frank again in his suite at the Sands.

"You're not going to believe who you're going to meet tonight at the show," Frank said as I watched him fix himself a drink.

"Who?"

"A real good buddy of mine from New York, Jilly Rizzo, and his wife, Honey. Jilly owns Jilly's on Broadway in New York. I've known them for a long time. Come to the show tonight, and I'll have you sit with them. You'll love them."

"Okay. I better go home and get dressed."

A few hours later I returned in a gorgeous red evening dress, with matching shoes, lace gloves encircled with diamonds and my gold charm bracelet. Nick Kelly, maitre d' of the showroom, showed me to a table in front of the stage, where Jilly, Honey, Annette, and another gentleman were sitting. Annette introduced me to Jilly, who had a pit-bull face and warm, gentle eyes, then Honey, a woman who didn't mince words. I sat down.

A few minutes later, the lights went down and the Rat Pack came out on the stage to sing. Just before the end of the first song, the audience turned to the back of the room. I turned too and saw Marilyn Monroe standing in the doorway in a long white gown decorated with flashy beads. The very large Nick Kelly escorted Marilyn down the aisle to our table. She sat in a chair next to me with all eyes upon her. The Rat Pack seemed stunned but continued to sing.

When they finished, Frank introduced Marilyn. I thought she was beautiful, though a little fuller in the hips than I had imagined. Marilyn shook my hand as Jilly introduced her to me. She said, "Pleased to meet you, Janie," in her wispy voice.

After the show, Marilyn stayed a few minutes to talk with Frank; then she was escorted from the hotel.

Dean, Annette, Sammy, Frank, and I walked to the Regency Restaurant for dinner. We were seated in the center booth. Frank ordered everyone shrimp cocktail, and we relaxed, sipping our drinks. No one bothered the celebrities when they were eating.

Through dinner, Sammy left the table for phone calls or had the phone brought to him. He dialed a number, mumbled into the phone for a few minutes, and hung up.

Finally, I asked, "Sammy, who in the world are you calling every thirty minutes?"

"I'm calling my wife. We're going to have a baby." He was married to May Britt at the time, and she was pregnant with their first child.

She was due in a month or so, and Sammy was a caring, attentive man. Obviously he was excited about becoming a father.

Annette had known Frank, Dean, and Sammy for years. When Sammy came back to the table after calling his wife, he said, "Annette, we're having a baby shower in a couple of weeks. Would you like to come to Hollywood for it?"

Turning, he said, "Janie, you're invited too, if you'd like to come."

Both Annette and I thanked Sammy for the invitation, but I bowed out: "Of course, I'd love to come, Sammy, but I don't know May, and I don't know if she'd want me there." We'd been drinking for hours, and none of us was feeling any pain—I wasn't sure how much the invitation really was intended.

"That's not important. Hell, the more, the merrier," he replied.

As a matter of fact, neither of us went.

After dinner, Frank, Sammy, Dean, Annette, and I went to Frank's suite at the Sands. It had two bedrooms, a large sitting area, and a wet bar, where we gathered, Frank playing host. A big bowl of matchbooks sat on the living-room floor. They were from restaurants, bars, and casinos around the world. Frank smoked like a train in those days, and I suppose he wanted cigarettes and a way to light them within reach at all times.

After a few drinks, Sammy and Dean went to their rooms, and Frank dismissed George, his valet, for the night. That left Frank, Annette, and me. Frank invited us to join him in the bedroom.

"Let's get comfortable, dolls," he said as he sat on the bed and took off his shoes. Then he undid his tie and unbuttoned his shirt. He sat in a chair, holding his favorite drink, Jack Daniels. "Hey, we're going to have us a little party! Annette, are you going to call those other broads?"

"Sure, Frank, just a minute." Annette steered me into the master bathroom and instructed: "Frank's going to want to party now, Janie. You get ready. Wash up or take a shower if you want. Make sure you're

149

fresh. Fix up your makeup and your hair, and put on some perfume. Everything you need is in here. I'm going to call some girls, and they'll be here in a few minutes. Be ready when they get here."

Within fifteen minutes there was a knock on the door, and I heard her answer it. By then, I had taken a shower and was dressed only in my panties, bra, black stockings, heels, and garter belt. When I came out of the bathroom, the party had just begun.

There were now four other women in the suite—Laurie, Audrey, Patsy and Annette, each of them topless, wearing sexy panties and garter belts. I had never met the others, but I learned later that they were some of the top hustlers in Las Vegas.

That night I learned that Frank loved seeing women making love to women, and he wanted to be right in the middle of it. He was in heaven. He took off his shirt and unzipped his pants, removed them, folded them carefully, and put them on the dresser. Now he wore only his briefs. "Come on over here, Janie," he said, motioning to the bed.

I lay down, and Frank told the girls to kiss me all over; they did what he wanted. I didn't know whether to scream, laugh, or what. This was the first time I had had sex with a woman, let alone four of them, and I was shocked and terribly nervous. Inside, I felt reluctant, but I knew that if I was to be accepted, I had to go along. I had no idea celebrities wanted this kind of sex, but here I was, in the middle of an orgy with Frank Sinatra. I moaned and groaned but was not turned on at all. I was scared.

At the side of the bed, Frank stood smiling, enjoying our performance, touching and feeling everything he could. I was trying to be cool and professional, but it was hard to detach from the scene. If that wasn't enough, I was in for an even bigger surprise. From between the arms and legs of the girls, I got my first good look at the real Italian stallion.

I gulped, "My God, Frank, what am I supposed to do with that thing? Throw it over my shoulder and burp it?"

"I'll show you what I want you to do with it." He jumped into the orgy on the bed.

The girls were licking my legs and sucking my breasts, and Frank said, "I'm going to lie beside you, baby."

I seemed to be at the center of the action. Everyone was making love to me. I was a very young twenty; they were all much older. Frank got under my body and tried to put his penis in my rectum. I screamed and said, "Oh God—that hurt me!" Then I reached behind his neck and scratched him.

I jumped up and ran to the bathroom. He thought because I was there with the other prostitutes I wanted whatever he wanted. But I ran to the bathroom, crying.

Afterwards, Frank paid the girls and they left; only Annette and I were still there with him. I jumped in the shower and scrubbed as hard as I could, trying to wash away the experience. I was disgusted that I let these people lead me into something I felt so repulsed by. I knew that to make as much money as I could I would have to go along with what my tricks wanted, but I never thought I would go this far.

After a few minutes, Frank came to the bathroom door. "Janie, are you okay? Are you coming out?"

"I'll be right out, Frank. Just give me another minute." I dried off, put a towel around me, and touched up my makeup. I looked at myself in the mirror. "You've got to get back out there and be the person he wants you to be," I told myself. I couldn't lose sight of why I was doing this. I took two more diet pills and returned.

When I came out, Annette had gone, leaving just the two of us in the suite. Frank took me by the hand and led me to the bed: "You don't look like you're feeling too good, honey. Why don't you come on over here and cuddle up with me?"

I think he understood I was upset. I climbed in and lay on my side. Frank curled up beside me, spoon fashion, his arm around me—his hand holding my breast. In a few minutes, he was sound asleep.

Late in the morning, Frank awoke, turned on again. He really liked sex and pretty, young girls. I did my best to make him happy. When it was over, Frank lay back on the pillows, a big smile on his face: "Oh, Janie, you are the best. I don't know who taught you how to do that, but I want you to thank him for me if you ever see him again."

I just grinned, got up off of the bed, and went to find my clothes. Frank dozed for a few minutes while I dressed; then he got up and put on a robe. He walked me to the door, kissed me on the cheek, then put his arm around me, and with the other hand slipped a wad of bills into my bra.

"After the show, meet me in the Regency Lounge," he said. "I want to see you again."

I thanked him for the evening. He kissed me again, on the cheek. I never let men I was doing business with kiss me on the mouth. It was an unwritten rule of the profession.

I went out the door, excited that I was going to see him again. On the way to my car, I pulled out the wad of bills and counted my earnings. Frank was generous, and I had made a haul. This would help fill my savings account for my daughters.

Late that night, I went back to the Sands to meet Frank. As I passed through the lounge, I saw Sammy, Dean, and Annette seated at a table near the front. The area was roped off again; small groups stood to the side, watching them. Sammy waved to me to join them, and as I was seated, ordered me a drink.

"Where you been, doll? Frank's been asking about you," he said.

"Oh, I just had to take care of some things." I wasn't ready to explain that I had spent a good part of the day shopping.

"Frank's out in the casino. Let's go harass his ass!" Dean said.

The four of us walked through the casino until we saw a huge crowd in the area near the blackjack tables. People were straining to see over and around the crowd, laughing and yelling at something in the center. Dean pushed through the crowd. There was Frank, dealing blackjack to a group of five pleased and surprised customers. He was having a ball, acting crazy.

"Hey, Frank, why don't you get a real job?" Dean yelled. "They need someone at the crap tables."

"Oh yeah, then I'll just move over there," Frank returned. He looked over and waved. "Hey Janie! Come on. Let's play some craps."

Frank handed the deck to the dealer, slipped him a chip or two, and walked toward the crap tables. We caught up with him, and he squeezed me as we tried to fight our way through the people. The crowd moved with us. By this time, four or five security guards were holding people back so we could walk with no one bothering Frank, Dean, or Sammy.

The three of them were crazy at the table. Frank grabbed the stick from one of the stickmen and started doing his job. Sammy and Dean were cutting up, throwing hundred-dollar chips on the table, not caring where they landed. Frank pushed the dice with his stick before the roller even had a chance to roll the dice. The people around the table were going nuts! I could see the pit bosses gathering to one side, watching the action. I don't think they were pleased.

Finally, Frank tired of the play and handed the stick to the stickman. "Thanks, buddy, we had a ball." He handed over a couple of chips. "Now that you know how to do it, see to it that you do it right. Give these people a break," he kidded.

The stickman smiled. "Thank you, Mr. Sinatra. I'll give it my best."

"Let's go have a drink," Frank whispered in my ear, "At my place. I gotta get outta here. Come on, doll." Frank guided me back through the crowd as fast as he could. The guards cleared a path as we walked toward the exit. Sammy, Dean, and Annette disappeared.

The public and the press just wouldn't leave Frank alone. They watched every move and constantly hounded him for autographs, interviews, and pictures. Frank sometimes lost his temper with photographers and reporters, his behavior almost always blown up in the media. Mostly bad things were printed about him, but he wasn't a bad person. Frank just wanted to be himself, and he was frustrated by the constant attention. I felt he was a lonely man. And when we were alone, he said so.

When we got to his suite, Frank mixed me a drink, and we relaxed for awhile. Then he got horny again and asked me to take off my clothes. "I want to see those pretty boobs again," he said, unfastening my bra.

Then Frank took off his clothes, and when he removed his briefs I could see I was going to be in for a stretch. I went into the bathroom to wash up. I put on a little perfume, then took my diaphragm from its plastic case. I figured I might need it that night. When I came out, he half-dragged, half-carried me to the bedroom. We collapsed on the bed, laughing.

Frank was gentle as we made love, and after about ten minutes, he was satisfied. Many months before, I had learned to fake an orgasm, and, like most women, I was pretty good at it. I gave him one of my best performances. Then I took him around the world, kissing every part of his body, spinning him over and over with my tongue. He shouted his pleasure: "Oh yeah!" Afterwards, we had a cigarette and a drink, climbed back into bed, and he cuddled me until we both fell asleep.

The next morning, Frank was returning to Las Angeles. He woke me saying it was time for him to get ready. I dressed quickly as he lay there, kissed him on the cheek.

"Thanks, doll," he mumbled. "There's something on the dresser. Take it and get yourself something pretty. I'll call you when the movie's done. I'll always call you when I'm in Vegas. You're the best."

I gave him another peck and left. I had no idea our gig would continue, but those two weeks were the beginning of a friendship of several years. Frank's schedule of appearances usually took him to

Las Vegas once a year, sometimes twice. My relationship with him remained solid for the nine years I lived there. Frank always got ahold of me or I called him when he was in town. Sometimes he was in town for a week-or-two gig at the Sands, and I was at his side whenever he wanted.

I met many show-business personalities after that first experience with the Rat Pack. I never slept with Sammy—white chicks didn't go to bed with black guys in the early 1960s, and I didn't think of him that way. We were friends. I was in Frank's suite one morning when I heard Sammy talking to Dr. Martin Luther King about the black movement. Sammy was pretty worked up. He stomped his feet on the floor at the end of the bar, and I could hear him saying that people would have to stick together about any decision they made. Sammy was easy to like. Frank just loved him. So did the others in the Rat Pack.

I never did much with Joey Bishop. He didn't like to drink or kid around. His didn't seem to fit with the rest; his humor seemed more dry and serious. He wasn't much with the Pack during its heyday at the Sands. Maybe he simply was true to his wife. He was there for the filming of *Ocean's Eleven* in 1960 but not when the Pack took the dealers' spots at the blackjack tables.

I know the guys gambled away tons of money, and the Sands let them do it. I remember sitting in the lounge with Annette, watching Frank and Dean heading to the tables, the people crowding around. The two guys loved to take over and entertain the people on the floor.

Later, through Frank, I met and tricked Sammy Cahn, the songwriter responsible for much of Frank's material—songs like "My Way" and "New York, New York." Frank told me Cahn wrote "High Hopes" for JFK's presidential campaign.

I got a call from George, Frank Sinatra's valet, seven months into 1961: "Frank is going to be in town in a few hours, and he wants you to come down to the Sands to meet him as soon as you can get there."

"Okay, George. Thanks." In short order I shopped for a new dress and shoes, headed to Colonial House to have my hair and nails done, returned home to dress, and drove to the Sands. Once there, I called Frank's room; George said he would be back in a few minutes and told me to come up to Frank's suite in Churchill Downs. All the buildings at the Sands were named after racetracks.

I was having a drink at the wet bar when Frank walked in.

"Hi, there, babe. How you doing'?" Frank kissed my cheek.

"I'm doing just fine now that you're back in town," I said, smiling about the money I would make.

Frank motioned towards his bedroom, and I followed. We lay there for nearly an hour talking about his collection of trains. He said he was getting his house ready for a visit from John F. Kennedy.

"That will be cool," I said.

Frank said how lonesome he was and that he'd enjoy my coming to see his house.

"I'd love to come there whenever you want me."

He told me he'd been written up in headlines regarding his actions with people he'd never even met. The papers lied about him he said; the newsmen never let him be. I felt sorry for him.

"I just want to be alone," he said, "to have my own thoughts and not worry about anyone else."

"I understand how you feel. Men always stare at me. I never go anywhere that a man doesn't try to pick me up," I said.

Frank lit a cigarette and asked me to make him a drink. He said I made him laugh a lot. Sometimes I danced around the room, doing splits for him, wearing only a garter belt and panties. He loved it.

Frank looked at the clock, then jumped out of bed and put on a robe: "Jesus Christ, it's 3:30 in the afternoon! George will be here any moment to line up my clothes for the evening show. Baby, get yourself washed up and out to the living room. You can talk to me while the manicurist is here."

I wrapped up in the top sheet from the bed and tiptoed into the bathroom thinking, "A man getting a manicure? I never knew a man who got his nails done. I can't wait to see it." I showered, fixed my makeup, and put on the dress I'd worn the night before. I sauntered into the living room in high heels.

"Get some coffee and sit down, babe!"

I got a cup of coffee from the bar and refilled his cup. The manicurist had rolled in a little table containing the tricks of her trade. Frank sat in his robe in a armchair with his right hand on the service table, while she sat across from him on a stool, a woman in her fifties, gently grooming one nail at a time, trimming each cuticle, filing each side of the nail down, and then buffing them all before applying a thin coat of clear polish.

All the while, George, a genteel black man in his forties, Frank's gentleman's gentleman, was busy in the bedroom picking up his clothes for the cleaners, straightening up the room, laying out Frank's clothes for the evening show.

When the manicurist finished, an older, sophisticated barber, dressed in a white double-breasted shirt and black dress pants, arrived with a tray and precisely trimmed Frank's hair, then carefully applied shaving cream to his face, and shaved his whiskers with a sharp razor. Frank sat back in the chair, relaxed, a plastic throw tied at his neck.

"You are so spoiled, Frank!"

"Yeah, right!" To him, the routine was simply boring.

After the barber left, I grabbed my purse. Frank stood up, handed me a wad of money, and said, "Meet me in the Regency Lounge for dinner at seven."

"Okay, Frank." I drove back to my apartment, called the beauty shop, changed clothes, put on a hat, and walked to the Colonial House Hotel.

The girls at the shop loved listening to tales of Frank and me while they did my nails and washed, set, and styled my hair. A few hours later, I hurried back to my apartment and put on a black evening dress with matching shoes, a lot of gold and diamonds over my white-satin, elbow-length gloves.

I drove back to the Sands and waited for Frank at a table in the Regency Lounge for about an hour. Then Dean Martin strolled into the room followed by Sammy Davis Jr. and Peter Lawford. The security guard immediately roped off an area, and everyone sat down. Sammy saw me across the room, waved, and yelled, "Janie, come on over here."

Everyone in the lounge turned to look at me. I smiled and walked through the entrance to join them. The guys stood up, and Sammy introduced me to Peter. I shook his hand, and he seemed to like what he saw. Minutes later, Annette promenaded into the room in an elegant dress, decorated with diamonds and pearls at her neck and wrists. We all had a drink before Frank walked in smoothly, capturing everyone's attention.

A crowd gathered behind the ropes, and fans reached out with paper and pen, trying to get autographs. Frank's bodyguard, a tall, solid man in his thirties, stood nearby, asking the fans not to bother Frank.

Peter finished his drink and left. The rest of us walked into the Supper Club towards one of three large booths at the center. A grand display of flowers dressed the circle. We crawled into the left black-leather booth; Frank sat in the middle, with Annette on his left and Dean next to her. I sat on Frank's right with Sammy on the other side. The table displayed a full setting of silverware, gold-plated white china, tall wine glasses, red roses, and glowing candles.

While we sipped our drinks, Frank ordered shrimp cocktail for everyone. The waiters brought tiny bowls sitting on a saucer—what I thought was soup—with a delicately rolled, white cloth placed directly next to the hors d'oeuvre. After eating the shrimp, I put the saucer with the bowl in front of me, then took the napkin and put it on my lap. Looking at the dinnerware, I picked up the outer spoon, which

I had learned from charm school was the proper order, scooped up a spoonful of soup, and sipped it.

"Janie," Frank whispered into my ear.

"What?" I said as Dean, Sammy, and Annette began to crack up.

"That's not a soup bowl. It's a fingerbowl. You're supposed to put your fingers in that bowl and rinse them off and dry them off with the warm towel they gave you."

"Oh my God! How embarrassing!" I quietly freaked out. There I was with the entertainers of the world, trying to drink the fingerbowl.

"That's okay, honey. Nobody saw anything except us!" Frank comforted me. He ordered me a New York steak that looked like half a cow. I ate about five bites and then watched them put it away. After the meal, I followed Frank to his dressing room, where I read his telegrams before being escorted to the table in front of the stage of the Copa.

With the house lights down and a spotlight on Dean, he opened the show with, "Strangers . . . in my room . . . how'd all these strangers get into my room . . . " Then Sammy and Frank came out to sing "Come Fly with Me." After the performance, Frank invited us to his suite for drinks. We gathered around the bar, and as Frank did the honors, we wandered into the living room.

Sitting there on the couches, we talked until Dean went behind the bar, then came walking up, asking, "Cocktails anyone?" He held a silver service tray in front of the white tails of his shirt pulled through his open fly. On the tray, a bar towel partially covered a roll of summer sausage surrounded by cocktail wieners and crackers. We roared.

"Get that thing outta here," Frank said, laughing.

It was close to 5 A.M., when Dean decided that he wanted some lovin', so he and Annette went to his room; Sammy left too.

I stayed with Frank and we did our usual play before nodding off.

19

I took a table at the Desert Inn, the first one in the front at the entrance to the lounge, and ordered a drink. One of the bosses, Aaron Weisberg, sat at the table next to mine, then asked me to join him.

"Did you see all the crazy golfers running around in here?" he asked. At that moment, a man of about forty walked into the lounge, towards us.

"Oh, my God! It's Sam Snead," I said.

"Hey, Sam," Aaron waved his arm. "Come on over and join us."

Sam sat down, ordered a drink, then: "Who's this cutie?"

"This is Jane Harvey. She's our little baby Jane," he said to Sam.

"Honey, do you play around?" Sam asked.

"We're in Vegas. Everybody plays around," I laughed.

Sam told us stories about funny things that had happened on the golf circuit. He kept us laughing until our sides hurt.

Then he asked: "Did you come out and watch us today?"

"I've never been to a golf tournament, but I'd love to."

"Well, make sure you're out there tomorrow when we tee off," Sam said.

"Oh, I will be. I'll be there with bells on."

"Is that all you'll wear? Bells? I won't be able to play the game." Sam winked. "Say, you want to come up and see my etchings?" (Lots of guys really did use that line.}

"Honey, I'd love to." I knew I'd hooked a big one.

Sam told me to meet him at his room down the hall from the casino. I said goodbye to Aaron, picked up my bag, and headed there.

"Get in here, quick! I don't want anybody seeing you," Sam whispered, opening the door. He was a married man, cheating on his wife. He called room service for a bucket of ice and a bottle of scotch. While we waited for it, he said, "Why don't you take off your clothes and stay awhile?"

I cracked up. I went to the bathroom to wash up and returned in only my black garter belt, hose, bikini panties.

Sam's eyes bugged. "You're quite a looker."

"You're not so bad yourself, honey," I said, just to be nice. I thought he looked waaay old.

Room service brought up the goods, and we had a drink. All this time, Sam kept staring at my breasts. Soon, he went into the bathroom; he came out a few minutes later, wrapped in a towel. I knew right away what he wanted, and I took him around the world.

Afterwards, Sam smiled from ear to ear. "I couldn't take much more of this. I wouldn't be able to play tomorrow. Can you stay the night?"

"Sure," I said, eyeing the gift he had laid near my purse, "but it will cost you more than *that*."

"No problem," he said as he pulled more cash from his pants on the chair next to the bed. We watched television awhile, then fell asleep.

The next morning, Sam showed me some of his golf swings and explained some of the ins and outs of the game. I enjoyed hearing about the finer points from a pro. He was attentive and kind.

"If you don't want to go home this morning, Janie, you can go pick yourself up a little dress in the hotel and sign my name," Sam said. "Meet me by the pro shop in an hour and a half."

He showered and dressed, preparing for the tournament he would play that day. I went to the dress shop and bought an outfit, a pair of flats, and a big picture hat. "Just charge it to Mr. Sam Snead," I told the woman who waited on me. Then I changed in the shop's dressing room, putting my other clothes in a fancy shopping bag, which I carried to the pro shop. Later, one of the caddies took it to Sam's room, so I wouldn't have to carry it on the course.

I followed Sam around the course. It was a beautiful day, but the desert was hot, and I was tired by the time the match ended. I met Sam by the pro shop again, and he told me to meet him in the lounge. He was back in a half an hour. We had drinks, and Sam introduced me to some of the other golfers in the tournament. They were all friendly.

"Baby, I have a proposition. Do you like fur coats?" Sam asked.

"Oh, I love fur coats. I think they're beautiful. But I don't have one."

"Well, you just might get one . . . " he said, mysterious. I was all ears!

He proceeded to say that he wanted me to keep one of his competitors, Arnold Palmer, out all night. He wanted me to wear Arnold out so that he couldn't play well the next day. Sam pointed him out: "There he is, sitting over there, the one in the blue shirt."

Sam wondered whether I could do it, and I assured him I could.

"I'll be back in a few minutes. See if you can talk to him," Sam instructed.

I went to Arnold's table and asked him for his autograph.

"Sure, honey, I'd be glad to," he said, signing the cocktail napkin I handed him.

I smiled shyly and thanked him politely. Back at my table, I flirted with him across the room. I could tell he was interested.

A pit boss sat down at my table. We talked for a few minutes about the entertainers appearing in Vegas that week. He waved over a friend and introduced Wilber Clark, owner of the Desert Inn, who seemed nice. Wilber didn't stay long, and soon I was alone again with my friend.

Not for long. Arnold soon joined us, talking about that day's match with the pit boss and me. I looked up at Arnold, smiled, and invited him to sit. The two talked on about the tournament while I just listened. I didn't mention that I had been out on the course watching Sam play. I could see Arnold sneaking looks at me as they talked, and occasionally he smiled—I suppose to keep my attention. He didn't know just how much attention he would get!

When the pit boss left, Arnold bought me a drink, saying he'd like to get to know me better.

"We'll get to know each other real soon," I said.

"Where can we go?"

"Down the street to the Colonial House Motel," I said. "You pick up some booze and meet me in about twenty minutes." I got my car, checked into a room at the motel, and waited for him to call me from the desk.

Twenty minutes later, the phone rang. I gave Arnold the room number, and he was on his way with a paper bag full of munchies and booze. He sat down, and I made drinks. I could see he was nervous, and I tried to make him feel comfortable by laughing at his jokes. He had no idea that Sam Snead was fronting this whole affair, and he didn't seem to realize I usually did this for a fee.

Arnold told me about golf, how he loved the competition, the chance to show his talent. After about four drinks, he said, "Why don't we get comfortable, Janie?"

I suggested we take a shower, and Arnold was hot for the idea. We stripped off our clothes and climbed in together. I washed his back, and he washed mine. We played for awhile before drying off and diving for the bed. He went at it hard, almost crazed. He wanted to do it all night long, and I made sure he did. Arnold was an interesting guy—macho, aggressive in bed, but sweet and gentle before and after—an excellent lover.

At some point, he noticed that the sun was peeking through the curtains. "I've got to get back to the hotel. I have a tournament to play!"

"Try to get some sleep before the game."

"It sure was fun, babe," he said as he dressed.

I dressed too and drove Arnold back to the Desert Inn. He asked me to come in for breakfast. After eating, we walked past the shops, and I stopped in front of a jewelry-store window to look at a beautiful pearl-and-diamond pinky ring.

"Do you like that?" Arnold asked.

"Oh, yes. It's beautiful."

He told me to wait outside the shop and walked in, then asked the clerk to pull the ring from the window. He returned with a gift-wrapped package and handed it to me.

"Thanks for the wonderful evening. Try to be in the lounge after the tournament. If I'm not tied up, maybe I can join you."

I drove back to my apartment and slept. That afternoon, I dressed in a sporty skirt and blouse and returned to the Desert Inn to collect my reward from Sam. I waited at a table in the lounge for Sam or Arnold, whoever showed up first. Sam joined me at the table.

After one drink, he said, "Well, you must have done a good job. Arnold's game was really off. I could tell he was tired. He must be up in his room now, sleeping it off. Did you keep him up all night?"

"Sure did." (I learned later that Sam won the tournament.)

"Baby, you sit here, and I'll be right back." Sam walked through the casino toward his room, returning five minutes later with a big box tied with a red bow.

"Here, Janie, I know you earned this," he said, handing me the box.

I opened it immediately. Inside was a gorgeous chinchilla jacket! I stood and slipped into it as if it were made for me. It fit beautifully. It was luscious. I gave Sam a big kiss on the cheek. "Oh, thank you very much! I just love it!" I whirled and twirled, showing it off.

"You look beautiful in it, and it looks beautiful on you," he said.

I sat down again, still wearing the fur. I was so excited about Sam's gift that I wanted to show him a fun time. "Why don't we go to my place? It's just behind the hotel. We'll walk through the golf course. That'll be fun."

"Okay, let's do it," said Sam. He was feeling no pain, having partied since the time the tournament ended. This was celebration!

We walked out of the casino to the golf course. It was late, but a full Vegas moon made the sky bright. Halfway across the course, I threw the chinchilla on the grass under a tree, fur side up, and lay down.

"Let's do it on the ground on the jacket you gave me," I giggled, just kidding around. But Sam was game. He got down on all fours, then lay on top of me, kissing my neck and caressing me.

"What if somebody catches us out here on the Desert Inn Golf Course with our pants down?" I said, realizing someone might see us.

"We'll give them a good show, Janie, and they won't even have to pay for it. My bare butt would be in all the newspapers, and it would be the first time anyone saw me with my hat off on a golf course!"

A half hour later, we got to my apartment, and I took him upstairs to my bedroom. In a flash, we were playing on the chinchilla jacket again. Sam was having a great time. I gave him a blow job, and he quickly fell asleep.

The next morning, he got up and, after arranging to meet me that afternoon at the Desert Inn, returned to his hotel. I went out later to have my hair done. At about five o'clock, I drove over to meet Sam.

He seemed to have been drinking all day; he was abrupt.

"Where have you been? You were supposed to meet me earlier this afternoon. You know, I didn't buy you that coat to have you traipsing all over town, showing off to other guys."

Taken aback, I showed him the pearl ring I was wearing and said, "Isn't this a pretty ring? Arnold Palmer bought it for me yesterday."

"Oh, let me see it." He took my hand, removed the ring, and threw it across the casino. "You know you're my girl now. I'm going to take you back to L.A., and you're going to be my mistress. I'm going to take real good care of you, and you won't be seeing anybody but me!"

"You son of a bitch. Nobody takes a ring off of my finger and throws it into the casino. That's my ring, not yours!" I ran into the casino screaming for the security guards and asking everyone seated at the blackjack tables to help look for my ring. I returned to the lounge without it, walked over to Sam, and pounded on the table.

"Who do you think you are, you asshole?" I stepped closer. "I kept my part of the deal to keep Arnold up all night, and you paid me for my services with that jacket."

Sam stood like a cock on a walk and, raising his voice, said, "When I gave you that jacket, I bought a piece of you."

I looked around the room, my face burning. "Nobody owns me! And nobody tells me what to do or when to do it!" I ripped off the coat and threw it across the table. All the drinks went flying. "If that's what you think, keep your lousy jacket."

Sam stood there with his mouth open as I stormed from the lounge.

I had the valet bring my car, and I drove to the Flamingo. After I settled down, I realized I'd just lost a pearl and diamond ring and thrown away a chinchilla jacket that I'd worked damn hard for.

I never let anyone pay me to trick someone else again.

20

One night I went to the Sands to have a drink at the Regency Lounge. Later that evening Nick Kelly, maitre d' of the Copa, introduced me to Mike Goldstein, a high roller from New York. I think he owned a fleet of taxicabs in the East. Goldstein bought me a drink or two, we went upstairs, and I gave him a blow job.

At the blackjack tables later, Mike told me he was going on a junket to the Bahamas. He asked whether I knew a couple of girls who could come along to take care of the fellows he was bringing with him. "Yes, I know some really good, trustworthy girls," I said.

When Mike and I proposed the junket, my friends—Laurie, Audrey, and Patsy—came to the hotel to talk about it. They thought it would be fun.

I had learned that two of the girls had "old men," or glorified pimps. An old man sits at home, takes care of the house, does the laundry, and generally runs the household. He is always there when his "old lady" comes home from hustling. He pampers her and cons her into believing he loves her so that he can control the money she takes in.

"Old men" are not sociable people. They don't frequent the hotels where their girls work, though they do go to the casinos while their girls are out hustling. They like to spend money, drive fast, pretty cars, and act important. Laurie and Audrey both told me their old men were excited about the junket because of the thousands of dollars they could make in a few days.

I didn't have an old man, nor did I want one. That made me an "outlaw"—up for grabs. The pimps looked at me as prime pickings, just waiting for an old man to con me into believing I needed someone to take care of me. I was hooked on this life for the big money, but I wasn't about to let anyone control me or tell me how to spend what I made.

At any rate, Mike said the four of us could make a lot of money. We told him we wanted two thousand dollars each up front, plus airfare and hotel. After talking another couple of hours, we all left the lounge, and Mike and I went back to the casino. He gave me some money and we played baccarat, first there at the Sands. We ended up at the Dunes, which kept the table open for him until 6 A.M. Then we agreed we needed some sleep. I went back to my apartment to count the cash he'd staked me—plus my winnings.

The next night, I met Audrey and Laurie at the Desert Inn. Audrey had auburn hair styled in the huge ringlets popular in the 1960s. They were piled at least a foot high on her head. She had a good figure, and she carried herself with assurance. I had met her earlier at the orgy with Sinatra. We had drinks in the Sky Room and made plans for the junket. I had the cash from Mike, so I booked our seats for the Bahamas.

The next Friday, Laurie, Audrey, Patsy, and I flew from Las Vegas to Florida and then to Grand Bahama. Once on the ground and through customs, we took a cab to the Lucaya Beach Hotel. We checked into a room with two king-size beds and a view of the ocean. It was just beautiful!

Later we met Mike in the bar with about fifty of his buddies. They were all businessmen from New York who had flown there for a weekend of gambling. They were all dressed in black hats and cashmere coats, totally out of place in the hot Bahamas. They soon changed to shorts and flowered shirts.

I gambled for hours with Mike, while Laurie, Audrey, and Patsy turned tricks with the rest of the guys. I didn't see them for hours. Finally Mike wanted to go to a reggae bar; once there I did a mad limbo. I could bend like my mother, and everybody in the bar egged me on. Afterwards, Mike wanted to go back and play more craps.

"You're my lucky charm," Mike shouted over the noise at the "hot" table as a crowd gathered round. "Don't you leave my side, honey— not even for a minute!"

I was throwing the dice, and I was hot. Everybody at the table was making money, and I had everyone yelling, "Come on, seven; come eleven!" while I threw the dice across a table full of chips. When I rolled a seven or eleven on the come-out, everybody went nuts: "Way to go, Janie! Way to go!" I rolled for fifteen minutes until I "sevened out," and the roller following me threw a pair of snake eyes—the dice had gone cold. All the players picked up their chips and headed for the cashier.

Mike and I went back to the bar to join some of his buddies. Then one of the guys said I was a "knockout chick." He wanted to see me in a bathing suit.

"No problem. I'll go put my bathing suit on, get the other girls, and meet all you guys by the pool."

I whispered to Mike that I was going to put on a show for his buddies; he should make sure they were at the pool in ten minutes. "I'm going to go upstairs and get the girls, and we're going to josh around the pool in our bikinis." I went to get Laurie, Audrey, and Patsy.

We met Mike and at least forty of his friends at the pool, some distance from the three-story casino windows looking past the pool to the ocean. A full moon lit the swaying palms and flowered bushes around the pool; we could see and hear the waves pounding the shore below.

Laurie, Audrey, Patsy, and I jumped into the pool. We did a water ballet with some handstands, showing our butts above the water. Then we climbed out of the pool and onto the diving board. One by one we displayed our bodies, bending over to show the cleavage beneath our bikinis before jumping off the board. We squealed and laughed like a bunch of kids.

Finally, I said, "Why don't you guys throw some chips into the pool so we can dive for them?" Some of them did, and we dived, picking the chips from the bottom with our teeth. The four of us competed for the chips, and the guys loved it.

Then from the crowd a drunk yelled, "Take if off! Take it all off!" Soon they were all shouting for us to take off our bikinis.

I was standing on the diving board, and I could see people looking at me from the casino windows.

The guys kept yelling. "Take it off."

Finally, I responded. "Well, we'd better see some hundred-dollar chips coming this way!"

A handful suddenly flew from the crowd to the pool. I started to pull the strings on the top of my bikini, teasing the guys to throw more chips into the pool. Finally, I dropped my top and started pulling the strings on the sides of the bottom. It dropped onto the board. I picked up the pieces, threw them aside, and dove in.

Laurie and Audrey were in the pool already, and when they saw that I was naked, they took off their bathing suits too. We swam back and forth and dove off the board, gathering the hundred-dollar chips. Some of the men threw fistfuls of five- to twenty-five-dollar chips; we picked them up right and left from the bottom of the pool. The drunken men seemed all to be going crazy, and we loved it.

Suddenly, a huge, black security guard came walking out of the darkness to the pool. We stopped to see what he wanted.

"You girls get out of this area. The pool is closed. Get those suits on," he shouted. He told the guys to go back to the casino. The party was over.

The three of us grabbed our towels, wrapped ourselves, and ran to our room. We lay on the beds and laughed and laughed, counting our winnings. Then we dressed and went back to the lounge. Mike and his buddies were there, drunker than skunks, and they all applauded as we walked in. We promenaded, arm in arm, swinging our hips, smiling and waving at everyone in the lounge.

"You girls need a drink," Mike said, and we started another round of boozing and turning tricks. The guys were hot to trot after seeing us naked. I tricked with four guys that night and made a bundle.

At about 3 A.M., we four girls met back in the room. Audrey had some marijuana, so we each smoked a joint and talked about all the married men we'd tricked and how they cheated on their wives. I loved smoking pot. The diet pills had worn off by then, and the pot made me feel good, not energetic or lively like the pills. It made me giggle until my sides were sore. I felt warm and spacey. After an hour or so I was very hungry. I found a bag of chocolate-chip cookies and devoured the whole thing.

The other girls were almost as giddy, and they laughed and laughed at me. When we all came down a little, we talked and giggled about the guys, the tricking, and the money we'd made. I finally passed out at about 7 A.M.

A few hours later, a loud, hard knock on the door woke us all.

"Who is it?" I asked gruffly through the door. I had a gigantic, throbbing hangover, and the noise hurt my head. I was in no mood for company.

The man on the other side said, "Miss Harvey, the hotel manager wants to see you as soon as possible."

I put on some clothes, ran a brush through my hair, and walked to the manager's office in the lobby. Laurie and Audrey were sound asleep, and Patsy was taking a shower.

The hotel manager met me outside his office and asked me to come inside. He was a middle-aged American, and he looked serious. He peered at me grimly over a pair of horn-rimmed glasses.

"Miss Harvey, I regret to inform you that you and your girls will have to leave this island," he said.

"What are you talking about?"

"You know very well what I'm talking about." His back was rigid, his face hard.

"No, I don't."

"I'm talking about your display by the pool last night. We do not put up with that kind of action in this hotel. Nor do we put up with the other things you're doing here."

"You're acting holier-than-thou. I've seen your girls floating around the hotel. It's pretty obvious what they're up to."

"I don't know whom you're referring to, but whoever they might be, they live here on the island," he said.

"Yeah, you're taking care of your own. Right!"

He didn't respond to my comment. "You're not welcome here, Miss Harvey, and neither are your three friends." He signaled the end of the conversation.

I could see I wouldn't win the argument. "Well, you'd better arrange to get our tickets fixed so we can get out of here," I said.

"I'm already taking care of that. You ladies be out in front in an hour. The car will pick you up then."

"Thanks a lot," I snapped and walked out of the office, slamming the door.

I thought about what happened as I stormed back to the room. The hotel hadn't asked the guys to leave, but it had no problem kicking out four women. It didn't seem fair. If the men hadn't wanted us to do the stuff we did, we wouldn't even have been there.

Laurie, Audrey, and Patsy were astounded when I told them we had to leave, but they dressed and packed in a few minutes. In a huff, I called Mike (and woke him up), thinking he might have some influence and could get the manager to change his mind.

He was sympathetic. "I can't believe they would treat you like that," he said, still groggy. "I'm sorry, honey, but there's not much I can do. But I'll call you when I get back to New York."

We were doomed. There was nothing to do but leave the place with our heads up and our chests out.

Laurie, Audrey, Patsy, and I paraded through the lobby to the front of the hotel. We could hear people whispering, and a few pointed in our direction. It didn't faze us! We sashayed out of that fancy hotel like four beauty queens on a runway.

The hotel van was waiting, and the driver didn't waste any time. He drove at least sixty miles per hour, and we were at the airport in minutes. Someone couldn't wait to be rid of us. At the airport, the driver showed us our new tickets—first-class, the only seats left on the plane.

The driver unloaded our bags, showed us to the terminal entrance, and drove off in a cloud of dust. Twenty minutes later, four exhausted ladies from Las Vegas left Grand Bahama. Soon we were flying over the United States, back to Nevada. Not that we were aware of it—we slept all the way.

21

One morning in September 1961, Frank Sinatra and I were having coffee in his suite at the Sands. He said he was tired of traveling all the time, and he felt lonely. He seemed happy to see me for the first time in a year.

Frank ranted that he was done with Peter Lawford; Peter had lied about President Kennedy staying at Frank's house. After he settled down, he said, "I care for you a lot, Janie. I think you have a lot of class. You know, class is born in you, and not many people have that. And some people you think have it, don't have it at all."

I didn't say a word, but I could see his disappointment as he paced the floor. He must have been upset about Marilyn Monroe's death the month before, but he kept it inside. Frank never talked business with me, but sometimes he just seemed to need someone to listen to him: "Janie, you always make me feel better. And you make me laugh when you do your splits and cartwheels."

We continued to sip our coffee. He said he was going to be in a movie called *Sergeants Three,* filmed in Utah. Then the phone rang. It was Dean, ready to go to dinner at Luigi's, where we had reservations that night.

"We've been waiting for you! What the hell is taking you so long? Did it take that long to get your joint copped? Come on, palsy, we have a show to do tonight!" Frank yelled into the phone.

We joined Dean and my friend Annette on the walkway leading to the pool area. It was at least 100 degrees F. outside; the heat took our breath away. We were walking side by side until Frank, Annette, and I veered to the left as we came to the shallow side of the pool. Dean walked straight into the pool, swam across it in his expensive black suit, tie, and shoes, then climbed up the ladder and out the other side of the pool.

"What are you looking at?" he said.

Frank bent over laughing, and Annette and I roared. The two of them always tried to crack each other up; Dean had pulled another good one.

Dean walked ahead of us toward Luigi's. He never broke his stride, though he left a puddle with every step. Frank, Annette, and I walked arm in arm, laughing all the way. Dean was almost dry by the time we arrived.

When we walked into the restaurant, Dean removed his tie and jacket and threw them onto the bar. He must have known the owner, who stood there watching, cracking up. Dean asked him to dry his jacket, then wrung out a sleeve on the floor. Someone came to mop up. By this time everybody was watching the show. Dean asked for an iron, too; everyone in the bar was laughing.

The owner approached our table, and Frank explained how Dean got wet. Dean said it was a good way to sober up for dinner. The owner took his jacket back to the kitchen and draped it over an oven door to dry. Dean took the wet money from his pocket and began to iron hundred-dollar bills on the bar.

After Dean dried out a little, we ordered dinner. Frank and Dean had to hurry back to the Sands to do their show with Sammy.

Back at the Sands, Frank told Annette and me to have Nick Kelly seat us at the table in front of the stage. As Nick walked us to our table, I thought about how nervous Frank was before performing. He'd said his stomach was in his throat just before each show. I pictured him looking into the mirror every two seconds to make sure each hair was in place. But I knew the butterflies would be gone after his first song.

When Annette and I got to the table, Jilly Rizzo and his wife, Honey, were already there. Both were quite a bit older, but they looked like a million bucks in their diamonds and evening attire. I shook Jilly's hand, then Honey's.

"How did you get that beautiful mink coat?" I asked her.

"I fucked for it, the same way minks do!"

Annette and I almost died laughing—I didn't realize then what I'd said, how silly it must have sounded to Honey.

Soon the showroom lights went down, and the Rat Pack came out and started clowning around. My attention was mostly on Mr. Blue Eyes, and again he sang to me. When I met Frank backstage afterwards, he asked how it went and I said it was great. While he refreshed himself, I looked at the telegrams covering two of the three sides of his dressing-room mirror. I was impressed that so many people wished him good luck for his opening show, especially after he'd done so many.

We met everyone back in the lounge. The men were clowning around, and after a time Frank went into the casino to deal some cards. Peter Lawford disappeared, too, and I asked Dean what had happened to him. He whispered that Peter needed some attention upstairs: "Why don't you run up there and give him some of your lovely specialties?"

Dean gave me Peter's room number; I went to his suite and knocked on the door. He was nervous, I think because he thought someone would find out what he was doing. He was a very soft-spoken guy. We talked and drank. Then I had Peter lie on the bed; I rubbed his legs and back and danced around the room to help him relax.

I lay beside him, pulled his skivvies down, and took him around the world. He said no one had ever done it that way before, that he'd had a lot to drink, that Frank had talked about how great I was. I cleaned up and went back downstairs with Peter right behind, grinning ear to ear. I made a fistful of bucks on that deal—fast and easy.

As we walked into the lounge to join Jilly, Honey, Sammy, and Annette, Dean said, "She's something else, isn't she?"

"Yes, indeed," Peter said. "She's one of a kind."

"Holy shit, you got that right!"

No one ever seemed to care about whether I enjoyed it—I really never did.

At about 4 A.M., the group started to break. Peter finished his drink, called it a night, and returned to his room. Jilly and Honey retired, too. Frank, Sammy, Dean, Annette, and I went to Frank's suite to drink some more, though we were pretty well smashed already. About an hour later, I noticed Sammy and Annette had disappeared.

"Where did those two go?" I asked Frank.

"I'll bet if you look in that bedroom over there you'll find out."

I waltzed over to the bedroom door, half open, and looked in. Annette was naked, crouched over Sammy's face, holding onto the headboard with both hands. I ran back to where everybody was sitting at the bar.

"You're not going to believe what I just saw over there."

"Oh, I can believe it, but I don't want to see it," Frank laughed.

I had never seen a white woman having sex with a black man, and I was tempted to look some more. But then Frank said, pulling me towards his bedroom, "Come on, Janie, I need you to rock me to sleep."

"Yeah, I'll rock you." I said. I gave him what he wanted and when it was over, I collapsed.

The next day I told Frank I had to go home. I dressed, and he kissed me on the cheek and said he'd call soon. I collected my gift from the dresser and left his suite. The Rat Pack finished its two-week gig at the Sands.

After resting for a day I went to the Dunes, where I ran into Sid Wyman in the lounge. He wanted to introduce me to one of his friends, a millionaire from Scottsdale, Arizona. I think his name was Marnell Lindsay Cougal. A tall elderly man with a big nose and receding hairline, he was homely as a mud fence but had a beautiful personality. That and his money made me love him. I soon forgot his appearance and just enjoyed him as a person.

Marnell loved to play baccarat. At that time, the casinos had a closing time and minimum and maximum limits on what a player could bet at baccarat. On certain occasions, the pit boss "forgot" the rules for special gamblers like Marnell.

After cocktails, we headed for the table. Marnell called to a friend walking through the casino. It was Abe Schiller, a Vegas boss and hustler. I remembered seeing him riding a beautiful horse in the Rose Bowl Parade in Pasadena. He and I hit it off right away, and the three of us went back for more drinks, joking and laughing the whole time. Finally, Abe had to leave, and Marnell and I went to the baccarat table.

As we sat down at the table, Marnell snapped his fingers. The pit boss came over and asked, "What can I do for you?"

"Bring me thirty," Marnell said.

Thirty thousand dollars! The boss then brought him three stacks of hundred-dollar bills, ten grand in each, and Marnell slipped me a short stack. He always played with cash. My eyes popped at all money on the table. Marnell threw out five or six thousand dollars in a hand. He won, then won, then lost, lost, lost. He was up and down all night, trying to get as close to a natural nine or eight as possible, playing against the house.

Spectators peered at us from behind the half-wall separating the main casino from the high-roller baccarat room. Heavily armed guards dressed in business suits overlooked the crowd from tall chairs, protecting the money on the table. The wait staff brought us whatever we wanted. No wonder—Marnell was throwing away hundreds of thousands of dollars! Every time he blew thirty thousand, he just snapped his fingers and said, "Bring me another marker."

I was winning thousands with the stake he provided, and I continued to play for three nights. For twenty-four hours, I left only to go to the rest room. On the second night, however, I told Marnell I just had to lie down for an hour. Even with the diet pills, I was getting tired. Besides, I thought if I got him in the room I could turn a trick and get over with it. He gave me the room key and said he'd be up in awhile. After a half hour or so, he came up, and I took care of him. When I said I had to go home, he answered, "You're my lucky charm. You can't go home. You're staying with me."

High rollers liked to have a beautiful woman on the arm, and Marnell was no exception. He insisted I continue to play baccarat.

I decided to stay and make as much money as I could. I took another diet pill, and we went back to the table. I ordered some food so that I could stay up and party. We gambled the rest of that night, into the morning, through the rest of the day, and into the early evening. I kept a smile on my face and kept up with his high energy. Finally, after three days of continuous gambling, he gave up. He lost a million dollars and didn't seem to mind.

We went to the lounge to have a drink. Sid Wyman was there, and when Marnell went to the rest room, I told Sid I felt sorry for Marnell but that his loss was good for the hotel. He told me not to feel sorry, that he'd seen Marnell gambling huge money for years. Sometimes he got lucky and won millions.

After Sid told me that, I decided to up my price and ask Marnell for more of the green stuff. Come on! I had spent three whole days with him. He gave me a ton of money for being at his side.

When Marnell returned, I gave him a kiss on the cheek and told him I had to go. This time he thanked me for staying with him and, without my asking, slipped me another wad of cash. I casually accepted his gift and happily walked from the casino knowing I'd made thousands with what he'd fronted me, a handsome amount for the trick, and a three-day bonus to boot! When I reached the apartment I took a sleeping pill, crawled into bed, and slept the next twenty-four hours. After that, Marnell always called me when he came to Las Vegas, and I was always ready to be his lucky charm.

Later that week, I went to the Sahara, and Jonesy, the pit boss, introduced me to Edward Platt. He played the part of the chief on *Get Smart,* a 1960s television show. Ed was staying at the Sahara, and when I met him later in the Casbah Lounge, he asked whether I'd like to go gambling.

"I'd love to—and I'm very lucky!"

"Well, I need some luck. Let's see whether some of it rubs off on me."

Ed was a personable, quiet man—warm and generous. I did bring him luck, especially at craps. We won hundred of dollars, and all night he handed me chips to play with and keep. Later, we went to his room, had a little sex party, and exchanged phone numbers.

"Call me at the studio if you're in Hollywood." Ed was now part of the growing collection in my little black book. I was with him a couple more times in Vegas, and I did see him in Hollywood when I was in California seeing my daughters.

After my divorce was final, I had made arrangements with Mae, my ex-mother-in-law, to see my girls in Santa Ana. Eventually she trusted that I wouldn't steal them away and allowed me to take them out without her. Probably the thousand I gave her every other month for the girls softened her. Neither she nor my mother and brother, to whom I gave diamond rings and gold bracelets, watches, leather jackets, television set, and more, seemed to care where I got it.

I drove to Santa Ana in my 1956 Thunderbird. Pulling up to Mae's trailer house, I'd hear her yell, "Get your things girls. Your mom is here."

Cindy and Roberta ran out to meet me. I jumped out of the car, and they threw themselves into my arms. I broke into tears, and they started crying, too. I held them tight, smelling their soft skin and hair. We went shopping and found beautiful clothes. Then I picked up some burgers and took them to a park to eat. I pushed them on the swings and they laughed; they made me feel so complete. But I knew that in a couple of hours we'd have to say goodbye, again.

Before we did, I gave them money to put in their banks and I gave Mae some cash. At the end of the day, we were sad and cried again. It was always that way.

"Please take me with you, Mommy. We want to live with you!" Roberta begged me, but Cindy seemed content to return to her father, who was still living with his mother.

After watching through the window Mae marched out, grabbed the girls' hands and pulled them back inside. Once they were in the house, I drove away. Often I had to stop and cry again. I promised myself I'd be back in a couple of weeks. I knew my daughters loved me and knew I loved them. But I was addicted to the Las Vegas money and life.

Instead of returning to Vegas immediately, I usually took a one-nighter at the Beverly Hills Hotel. I'd call Ken Hansen, owner of Scandia Restaurant to say I was in town before driving down for dinner. Scandia had been a Hollywood hotspot since 1954. I hoped to meet a movie star or high roller there. I wanted the big money. That's all I thought about.

Alone and dressed to kill, I sat at a table, ordered a drink, scanned the crowded bar, and recognized one face. At first, I couldn't place him, so I asked the waiter who he was.

"That's Johnny Weissmuller. You know—Tarzan."

I could hardly believe it. Johnny was a movie star and a world-class athlete. He'd won five Olympic gold medals in swimming. I walked right over and introduced myself.

"Hi," I said, placing my hand on his shoulder, "My name is Jane."

He held out his hand and said, "Hi, Jane. My name is Tarzan." Drunk and barely able to talk, he looked to be in his early sixties. I felt sorry for the hero—his face was flushed and his eyes looked yellow.

The bartender brought my drink, and Johnny entertained us: "When I'm swinging through the jungle, and when I swing over to you, Jane, you grab the vine, and we'll swing through the jungle together. So when I saw Jane, I swung over to her, and when she grabbed my . . . I screamed 'the vine damn it, the vine!'"

Everyone cracked up. Johnny continued, but after awhile a man came into the room, announced that the bus to Las Vegas was leaving, and Johnny left with a group.

I continued to sip my drink. The bartender brought me another, saying it was from the older, bald man sitting with three other men on the other side of the restaurant. I looked over, raised my glass, smiled, and nodded. He smiled back.

At almost the same time, Ken Hansen walked in from the main dining room. He remembered being introduced to me by Sid Wyman. Ken was not one of my johns, just a kind man I had met and talked with a few times.

"Who's that old man over there? He just sent me a drink?" I asked.

"That's Bill Frawley."

I must have given him a blank look because he laughed and said, "Don't you recognize him, Jane? That's Fred Mertz, from *I Love Lucy*. Now he plays Uncle Charlie on *My Three Sons*."

I stopped and stared, then: "Oh my God! I recognize him now!"

"Would you like to meet him, Janie?"

"Oh, yes! That would be fun."

I followed Ken to Bill Frawley's table. Bill invited me to sit and asked whether I'd like another drink. I was there for only a minute before he asked, "By the way, do you play around?"

"Sure, doesn't everyone?"

We sat and talked for almost three hours, drinking and watching the people in the restaurant. Every once in awhile, Bill pointed out some movie or television personality. Finally he asked whether I wanted to see his etchings. He was certainly direct.

I wondered, "Am I going to have to give this old fart a blow job or mouth-to-mouth resuscitation?" I liked Bill, and he was a lot of fun, but men thirty years older turned me off! Still, I had come here to make money, and he had some, so I went.

The valet brought Bill's car to the front, and Bill drove us to his apartment near Hollywood and Vine. It was a one-bedroom place, decorated simply but comfortably.

In his living room, Bill had a custom-made, wood coffee table with a glass top. We sat on the couch and looked through the glass to see photographs dear to him, from the *I Love Lucy* show. He explained who was in each one and when it was taken. The walls of the room were lined with other pictures of Bill with other celebrities he had known. I just loved looking at them and hearing about the times of his life.

After I turned a quick trick, Bill drove me back to the restaurant so I could get my car. Before we parted, he said he would take me to the *I Love Lucy* set the next day. I had never been to a television studio before, so I was excited about seeing it.

The next morning, we met at the Scandia for a Bloody Mary, and soon he asked whether I was ready to go. The guard greeted Bill at the entrance, then opened the gate, and Bill drove into Warner Brothers Studio. He pulled into his personal parking space in front of one of the sound stages, and we got out and went in the back door. It was huge inside! The black ceiling was filled with lights, and the sets were surrounded by scaffolds and wiring. It wasn't as glamorous as I'd imagined. It was a day off for cast and crew, so Bill showed me around the studio as well as some other buildings where shows were filmed. Then we went to the studio commissary, where everyone ate lunch.

On our way there, I saw a redheaded woman driving a golf cart. Bill yelled, "Hey, Lucy!"

Lucille Ball drove over to us and stopped the cart.

"Hey, Bill, what are you doing here? We're not shooting today," Lucy said, laughing. Then she looked at me and said, "And who's this little gal you have with you?"

"This is Jane Harvey," Bill said, "She's from Las Vegas." He turned to me and said, "This is Lucy."

I told her I was thrilled to meet her, and before she sped off she said it was nice to meet me too, I watched her red hair bouncing as she drove over the rough back-lot street.

Bill took me to see some additional sets, and two hours later we headed back to Scandia for a drink. Finally, I said I had to head back to Vegas. I promised to call him when I came back to Hollywood, and I did see him about five times between 1962 and just before he died in 1966. He liked me for me and I felt the same way about him.

22

A few months later, in February 1962, Frank came back to town. Annette called and said he and his friends were going on location to shoot *Sergeants Three*. She said to get my butt down to the Sands.

"Oh, boy! Frank's back in town!" I thought. "I can make a ton."

I dolled up in a new, black-sequined dress and showed up at the Sands, ready to party. In the Regency Lounge, I saw Annette standing at the bar, talking to a huge man. She introduced me to Dan Blocker—"Hoss" in the television series *Bonanza*.

"Frank asked me to watch over you girls sitting here in the lounge," Dan said.

"You sure are a big enough man to watch over us two little girls," I kidded.

Dan roared. Then into the lounge walked Lindsay and Gary Crosby, Peter Lawford, Dean Martin, Sammy Davis Jr., Joey Bishop, Johnny Rivers, and Frank. The hotel staff set up tables and chairs in clusters in the lounge, roped off almost entirely for them.

"Hey, have you been taking good care of my girls?" Frank asked Dan.

"You bet!"

Frank sat down with Annette and me, and we ordered drinks, the whole crew cutting up as always. The celebrity watchers were going absolutely crazy, seeing so many stars at one time, in one place. They didn't know that all of them were going on location in Utah.

Soon Annette and Sammy left, and Frank went out to the tables to gamble. Dean came over and whispered in my ear, "Why don't you come up to my room, baby? I've been wondering what Frank's been getting that I haven't. I'll see you in twenty minutes."

I waited for a few minutes, then went to his room. Dean was a calm, cool-headed guy, mostly quiet unless he was cutting up with Frank and Sammy. Always sweet to me, he wasn't then the drunk he portrayed. He just acted that way to get laughs. In later years, he *was* drunk, often working with a drink in hand. But all the Rat Pack partied on stage; the audience loved it and screamed for more.

I turned a trick with Dean and went back to the lounge.

"Where've you been?" Frank asked.

"I'll never tell," I laughed. But I often thought about how these men passed us working girls around like dessert trays. Sometimes I felt more like a strawberry cheesecake than a real person. I thought, "These guys fly into Vegas, see a pretty girl dressed to kill, take her to a room, get their jollies, go back downstairs and gamble, and probably don't remember her first name. They have sex with a complete stranger and then say, 'Pass the biscuits.'" I didn't realize I was doing the same thing—only I said, "Pass the cash."

I also wondered how, after spending thousands of dollars on some dame, these guys could go back to their wives and kids, hold up their heads, and look at themselves in the mirror.

I was at the table only a few minutes when Frank said, "I have a really great friend who's staying here. His name is Sammy Cahn. He's the guy who wrote "High Hopes" for me, the song President Kennedy used for his campaign." Frank said Sammy wanted a real fine lady to come up and see him. Frank gave me the room number, and I left the lounge again to take care of his friend . . . Just pass the hors d'oeuvres.

When I walked into the room, an elderly gentleman was sitting nude on the bed with a sheet draped over his lap.

"Come on in," Sammy said. "What's your name?"

I told him, and he invited me to have a drink. I poured myself some scotch on the rocks, then sat on the bed and talked with him. He was a nice, funny man, and I laughed with him at his jokes.

Then he said, "Get yourself comfortable," and I did, undressing in the bathroom. I turned a quick trick and in no time was out the door with a generous gift.

Frank was gone when I returned downstairs. Annette was having a drink with Lindsay Crosby, who was young and cute. I joined them, thinking it was a nice change to talk with someone closer to my own age.

Johnny Rivers walked to our table and sat down. He was just starting out, and Lindsay encouraged him to go out and do his own show. Johnny didn't think he had the right stuff to make it big in the music business, but Lindsay kept saying he was good, that he knew good talent when he saw it.

Then Lindsay leaned over and asked me whether I smoked pot. I told him I loved it, so he invited me to his room for a joint. There we had a drink and smoked a couple of joints. Lindsay loved my low-cut dress and commented on it several times. Then, "Are you one of Frank's gals?"

"Yes, I am."

"Tell me something. Would you charge me the same thing you charge Frank?"

"For you? If I didn't to have to make some money, I wouldn't charge anything." I meant it—he was that cute.

"What would I get if I gave you a C note?" Lindsay asked.

"Honey, what would you want?" I laughed.

"Let's get naked," Lindsay said, a gleam in his eye. So, we did. We chased each other naked around the room, stoned and drunk, acting like two teenagers. He was a lot of fun. After about two hours of romping, we had sex, and afterwards we both dressed and went back downstairs.

The casino was screaming with activity. Bucky Harris was going bananas in the pit, and when I walked over to talk to him, he said so. Nick Kelly came over, and we talked about the crowd and how busy the casino was. Then Frank came in, and I headed back to his table.

"We're getting ready to cut out. We're going on location in Utah," he said. "We have to leave soon. Do you want to go with me?"

"No. I better not." I was too drunk, too stoned, too tired. I wanted to go home and get away from the strip for awhile.

"I'll be back to do a show tomorrow night," Frank said. He kissed me on the cheek and said he'd have George call me when he got back. All of a sudden, all the guys in the lounge were gone, milling around with their bags in the front of the hotel . . .

Frank was back the next night, saying he had performed his own stunt on location, hanging beneath a runaway stagecoach.

"That was a crazy thing to do," I said.

"My insurance company's outraged!" He laughed.

When I saw Jack Entratter, the entertainment director at the Sands, that night, I asked how he was managing with all the big personalities there. He laughed and said the hotel was busting at the seams, going crazy night and day. Frank had said he was glad they were shooting in this part of the country because he could perform at the Sands and stay in one place for a change. Carl Cohen, a Sands owner, joined our conversation. He said he had heard I met Sammy Cahn—I imagine from Frank.

I told Carl and Jack about Sammy and what a nice man he was.

They both thought it was cool I had taken care of him, since he was in their age group and men their age loved pretty, young girls.

When I did well, as I did that night, I tipped all the people I knew in the casino, from security guards to blackjack and crap dealers, parking attendants to waitresses. I slipped twenty-five-dollar chips into their palms and told them I had had a good night. And I asked them about theirs. I was noted for good tipping—when I had a good night, everybody else did too. We all took care of each other then. It was a very small town.

About three weeks later, I got a call from Bucky Harris. He said he had a friend in town who would like to meet me. I got ready and went down to the Sands. I found Bucky in the pit, and he took me to the Regency Lounge. There, he introduced me to a man named Harry Karl. I learned later that he was the husband of Debbie Reynolds and that he owned Karl's Shoe Stores, a nationwide chain. We went through the usual routine. Harry took me gambling at the Sands, and then we hit a couple of other casinos. I was on a winning streak and so was Harry. He was happy I brought him such good luck.

Harry had three friends along hot to meet some girls, so I called Audrey, Annette, and Laurie. The eight of us went to see Judy Garland at the Sahara. Judy was having a hard time then, and she didn't have her usual pizzazz. She slurred her words and forgot lyrics. Some in the audience heckled her, which really upset me. I loved Judy Garland, and I thought their behavior was rude. She didn't even seem aware that anything was going on.

After the show, we went back to the crap tables and gambled some more. I introduced Jonesy to the guys, and they hit it off immediately. When we were all gambled out, Harry took me to his room, and I took him on a fantasy ride. He asked me to meet him the next day for lunch.

Getting out of the shower the next morning, I heard a TV newsman say that President Kennedy had been shot. I watched for about an hour until there was a newsflash that the president had died from a gunshot wound to the head. This seemed to me the saddest thing that had ever happened in America.

After awhile, I called Harry Karl at the Sands. He said he had to leave immediately, that some of his friends were acquainted with the president and wanted to return to Los Angeles. He said he would call the next time he was in town, to call him when I came to Hollywood. Six months or so later, I did see Harry again.

After talking with Harry, I went to the Thunderbird Hotel for the seafood bar. The waiters said the hotel was draping all its gambling tables and slot machines in black to mourn the president. The city was going to turn off all the lights, including those on the strip, for a long moment that night. That evening the lights did go off, and for a few seconds there was total darkness in Las Vegas. It was eerie. Nothing moved. All the people bowed their heads in prayer. I was so sad about our president's death that I didn't work for the next week.

23

One afternoon, I was to meet Audrey at the Flame Restaurant near the Desert Inn for dinner. I hadn't seen her since our trip to the Bahamas, so we had lots to catch up on.

I had a cocktail in the bar—all red, black, and gold, a 1960s modern kind of place. I waited at least an hour and a half, but Audrey didn't show up. I figured she must have caught herself a high roller. I filled the time laughing and cutting up with the bartender. I was getting a little tipsy.

Once, when I turned to light a cigarette, I noticed a man sitting at the other end of the bar, staring at me. He was thin, well dressed, probably in his early forties. He reminded me a little of Johnny Carson when he was young. I could see some muscle bulging through his sport shirt. I looked at him, and he looked at me, and I looked at him. Finally, he came over and offered to buy me a drink.

We exchanged names and pleasantries. He said his name was Johnny, that he was a pit boss downtown somewhere. I didn't tell him

191

much about myself. I told some things about myself to tricks, but this guy was not a trick. We had four drinks, and he asked me to go to a friend's house to smoke some pot.

"Yeah, let's go! Let's party!" I was happy to meet a man I was attracted to, who looked like he would be a lot of fun, not for business. He was handsome, had a nice body, and seemed to be attracted to me. I was lonely; I wanted a man who was not a trick to give me some real attention.

Johnny drove me in his white 1959 Cadillac—the model with the big fins to the rear, fun to ride in—to his friend's house. His friend Mike was home, and we all had drinks together. Then they brought out the pot, and we smoked several joints. I got the giggles and the munchies. Mike called to order a pizza, then left to pick it up.

Johnny made his move. All of a sudden, he was sitting close to me on the couch, looking into my eyes. A funny feeling came over me. I think I was attracted to him sexually, the first time for me, in a long time. Johnny put both arms around me, held me and kissed me. I felt like I had been hit by a bolt of lightning, and I returned his kiss. We sat and kissed until Mike returned with the pizza, which we ate in a short time.

Mike had to work later that evening, so he wanted to go to bed. Johnny asked me to his place for another drink. I accepted eagerly. Johnny's place was a trailer located a few blocks past Fremont Street, not far from downtown Vegas. It was small, but it had a kitchen, living room, and one bedroom. We didn't finish even one drink before we ended up in the bedroom. Johnny was an expert at lovemaking, and he went at it with gusto.

He drove me back to my apartment the next afternoon and asked me to meet him at the Flame Restaurant the next night. I didn't promise I would be there but that I would call him when I knew my plans. Actually, I knew I would be there to meet him. In fact, all I did that day and the next was think about him.

I fell in love again. I couldn't help myself. I wasn't interested in being with a man who cheated on me and I didn't want a man without a job. He seemed perfect. Someday I wanted to get out of the business, to lead a normal life. Being with someone I cared about seemed like a good start.

• • •

One night just before Christmas 1963, I was in the Sands Hotel talking to Nick Kelly, the Copa maitre d', when he said, "Have you seen Betty? She got her boobs pumped up!"

"What do you mean—pumped up?"

"Some doctor in town is putting something in them. It perks them right up."

I looked down at my breasts and pushed them up: "I need some of that stuff!"

"Oh, no you don't! You're perfect as you are! Seriously, Jane, you don't want to do that to your body. You never know what that stuff will do," Nick said.

"Yeah," I said, laughing, "I'll have nicer boobs, that's what!"

"Well, Jane, if you want to talk to Betty about it, she'll be in the cocktail lounge after the second show."

"Thanks, Nick." I gave him a big smile as I walked away.

At that time, in the 1960s, each of the hotels required two or three showgirls to sit in the cocktail lounge after their shows, to talk with customers for an hour or two. This was another game that the casino played to make people stay around longer and spend more money. The showgirls walked in wearing street clothes—as well as the three pairs of eyelashes they'd worn in the show.

The showgirls were elegant women who met strict job requirements, including an outgoing personality, a beautiful face with a perfect set of teeth, height of at least five-feet-eight-inches, and a fantastic body with voluptuous breasts.

Showgirls were a huge casino attraction. The minute someone

saw a showgirl walk into the lounge or casino, you'd hear someone say, "Oh, my God. There's a showgirl." Everyone would turn around and stare, as if they were goddesses.

At the beginning of each show, the girls walked onto the stage, balancing heavily decorated (and heavy!) headdresses. They wore beautifully designed—topless—gowns, their breasts exposed. They walked the stage from left to right with arms outstretched, the long trains of their gowns spread behind them. They posed for twenty minutes or so, ultimately glamorous. The presentation then was pure, elegant art.

Knowing Betty would be in the cocktail lounge that evening, I made sure I was there too. She gave me the doctor's phone number, and I called him the next day. I had just turned twenty-two, and my breasts were starting to droop, probably the result of having two children. I wanted my breasts to be as firm and attractive as Betty's!

The doctor was right down the street from the Sahara. An older man, popular with many of the girls on the strip, he authorized prescriptions for my diet and sleeping pills and provided other services that Vegas girls needed. During this visit, he checked my breasts and took my vital signs. Then he had me watch a slide show regarding silicone injection.

Afterwards, he said, "I've tested this silicone on my wife, more beautiful than ever. I've shot it into her breasts, her cheeks, the sides of her eyes, and her behind. I think you're going to be real happy with the results. It's safe and your breasts will still be beautiful, standing at attention, when you're eighty. You'll need only one injection to each breast. You'll see instant improvement." He left the room for a minute, then returned with an inch-wide, foot-long tube filled with raw silicone.

The doctor injected a local anesthetic under my breasts to numb the area and said, "Hold perfectly still while I inject this soft gel. You shouldn't feel a thing." Starting with my left breast, he inserted the two-inch needle and slowly pushed the stuff in.

"As the slides showed you, the soft silicone is placed within the sealed-off cavity in your breasts, which makes them feel naturally soft to the touch. You'll never have to worry about your breasts sagging again." He repeated the injection in my right breast. In ten minutes it was done.

When I sat up and touched my breasts, I immediately felt the change. I understood why Betty was happy with the results of silicone injection, and I was surprised at the simplicity of the procedure.

"Just massage them three times a day, or have your old man massage them, and everything will be okay," the doctor said, laughing.

My breasts felt a little sore for about three days, and after that, they felt fine. Now they looked as they had when I was sixteen. They were perky and full right away, and I felt sexier than ever.

24

After a weekend of Johnny's pampering, it was time to get back to work, so I had my hair and nails done, donned the Mr. Blackwell, slipped on high heels, and drove to the Desert Inn, hoping to find some high rollers.

As I walking into the cocktail lounge I noticed a handsome, itty-bitty guy with a tall, slender woman, sitting at one of the tables. They looked like they were having a ball, so I sat down at a table next to them. After ordering a drink, I looked over and asked where they were from.

"My name is Babs, and this is my husband, Willie Shoemaker," the woman said.

"You mean the famous jockey, Willie Shoemaker?"

"You got it. Why don't you join us?"

After a few more drinks, Babs said, "Let's go dancing up at the Sky Room!"

The three of us took an elevator to the Sky Room on the third floor tower of the Desert Inn. There a three-piece band performed before a small dance floor in the window-walled room overlooking the strip.

We danced and carried as if we'd known each other for years. After the two of them danced, Willie asked me to dance, reaching out to pull me from my lounge chair. Pulling me close, he nestled his face between my breasts as he guided me around the floor.

"Now you know why I love tall women," he laughed.

It felt odd to be dancing with a man so short, and I couldn't believe he was doing that to me in front of his wife. I turned to see Babs's reaction, and she just laughed. Of course, she didn't know that I was a hustler, but I would never have taken advantage of them. In fact, I had forgotten entirely about making money, having long since decided to spend the evening having fun with them.

Then Wilber Clark, owner of the Desert Inn, and his wife joined our table. Willie introduced me to Wilber, a charismatic businessman with thinning white hair in his early sixties, and his wife, Toni, a classy brunette dressed in a white evening gown with diamond necklace, bracelet, and earrings. I'd met Wilber just once, briefly, as he wasn't much for walking the casino in the way of owner Riddle at the Dunes.

Wilber asked whether we'd like to see *Hello, Dolly*. We loved the idea, so Wilber got in his Cadillac with Willie in the front seat beside him and the three women sitting in back. Thus we rode to the Rivera, where Betty Grable was performing. When we got to the front door of the Rivera, Willie jumped out of the car and opened the back door. I moved my legs one by one and put my high-heeled feet on the ground as Willie extended his right hand. I grabbed it with my white-gloved right hand, and he pulled me from the seat like a feather!

"God, Willie, I can't believe how strong you are," I said.

"That's from holding those horses back," he chuckled.

I looked at his feet. "I can't believe how physically strong you are for being such a small guy? Just look at your feet!"

"Honey, hold out your hand," he responded.

I did, and he laid his foot right in the palm of my hand. It reached only from the end of my middle finger to my wrist. I was blown away.

"Yeah, but he's larger in other areas," Babs laughed.

When we got to the showroom door, the maitre d' escorted us to the best seats in the house. While we waited for the performance to begin, Babs and I had the waitress spike Willie's drinks with a little extra alcohol. Willie seldom drank much, and I doubt he appreciated it.

After the show, Wilber drove us back to the Desert Inn. By that time I was exhausted and excused myself to go home. I called for my car and drove back to the apartment. Wilber Clark died in 1965 of a heart attack. Betty Grable divorced Harry James in October of that year.

All the shows were free to celebrities and casino owners, so I never had to stand in line and wait—a huge benefit. I ended up seeing *Hello, Dolly* five more times during the 1960s, with five different tricks. I often escorted johns to shows I'd seen before, always pretending it was the first time. I saw Engelbert Humperdinck (whom I tricked once), Tom Jones, Ray Charles, Aretha Franklin, Dionne Warwick, the Mamas and Papas, the Fifth Dimension, Elvis Presley, Don Rickles, the Supremes, Stevie Wonder, Ike and Tina Turner, Sonny and Cher, Fats Domino, and many other fabulous shows. Some were just lounge acts then, still hoping to achieve the stardom they eventually won . . .

I woke up late that afternoon feeling good about the night before. It was nice to be with a happily married couple for a change. I wanted to have a life like theirs, and I felt Johnny could be the man to make it so. I remember the first time he made love to me. I actually enjoyed it! He was understanding, gentle, and romantic. With him, I felt satisfied. He loved me for me!

I had been lonely, on my own, for nearly five years, and having a companion to share my feelings with was wonderful. Johnny listened to me when I needed to talk to someone. He rubbed my back and feet, and he ran a warm bubble bath for me after we made love.

I wanted to be loved, to have a family life, and to quit turning tricks—exactly what the phrase implies, that is, performance. No emotion or commitment expected, purely business for the girls, ego boost/pleasure for the johns, abusive in the long run to both, though I think only the women realize it. And they fool the men into thinking they enjoy it too.

At any rate, I wanted to look good for my second date with Johnny, so I had my hair done and spent a long time picking out a dress because I wanted him to feel the same way I already felt about him. I knew I had to be careful he was the right one. I prayed he would be the one, that he would love and support my daughters and me.

We had arranged to meet at the Flame Restaurant, so I drove over and strolled into the lounge. A trim forty-year-old with high cheekbones, a square jaw, and piercing brown eyes, Johnny looked twenty, totally seductive in his blue silk shirt and sport coat. He was sitting in a booth.

Johnny seemed excited to see me. He immediately rose and welcomed me with a hug and kiss. Shivers went up and down my spine. All through dinner, he sat and stared at me, saying I was beautiful. I told him the whole story of my daughters and how I had lost them to my mother-in-law. I hadn't said anything about them earlier because I wept just thinking about them, and I wanted to be happy for a change. But Johnny was sympathetic, understanding of my tears. He said he would do anything to help me, and that's what I wanted to hear.

Johnny said I was his kind of woman. He liked that I cared so much about my children, and he loved how I looked when I talked. He made me feel like a person who mattered. He was handsome physically and completely charming. He made me believe he loved me.

"I've been thinking about you since we met. I can't get you off my mind," he said. "I just want to grab hold of you and take you home and keep you forever."

When we left the restaurant, Johnny, very much the gentleman, opened the car door for me As we drove down the boulevard, I asked, "What hotel did you say you work for, Johnny?"

"Well, I don't work anywhere now. They laid me off down at the Golden Nugget. I was dealing there last week. You must have misunderstood me, honey," he said. I figured I had misunderstood because we had been smoking pot when he told me he was employed.

When we got to Johnny's trailer, we drank and smoked a joint or two and soon we were in bed. He kissed me from head to toe, like I did with the high rollers, which was absolutely wonderful. No man had ever treated me like that before: I had never had that kind of attention. I fell in love then and there.

After we made love, we smoked more pot and talked. My mind was cloudy, but Johnny told me he had been with other women, "women who worked in whorehouses." He said he was the kind of guy who stayed home and took care of the house and the money. This was the life he had lived since he was a young man in Philadelphia.

He said he had served three years in jail for taking a seventeen-year-old across a state line. The two had an argument and she called the cops from a gas station. He had spent another couple of years in prison for stealing cars, and then he met a woman named Dorothy, who worked as a prostitute in the brothels. The two of them had a daughter, and he stayed home to take care of her while Dorothy worked. Eventually he left and moved in with a younger prostitute. They moved to Vegas, had a son, and she left to take the baby back East.

Now he was looking for work, hoping to get a job as a pit boss at the Golden Nugget. He wanted to go straight.

I felt so sorry for Johnny. I wanted to love and take care of him, and I knew I could help him pay off his bills. "I'll show him what a high-class hustler can do," I thought. "He's never seen the kind of money I can make!"

As I listened to Johnny telling me about his problems, I dreamed my own dreams. I saw Johnny getting a real job, our working together to pay off his bills, then my quitting the profession and staying at home in a house (I still wanted a picket fence) where we would raise my daughters. Everything would be perfect—a simple life, like that of other married couples, happy families, full of love and trust. I would be able to give my girls something I never had—a chance to grow and learn without being afraid.

"I don't know what it is, but I think I could fall in love with you," Johnny said.

"Well, I *am* in love with you," I said.

We stayed together in his trailer for three days. I didn't turn any tricks; I didn't go back to my apartment. We took bubble baths together, drank champagne. Johnny cooked meals for me, and we made love any time, day and night.

Finally, I went back to my apartment to prepare for a night on the strip. I wanted to show Johnny how much I could make in one night. I'd give him cash to pay off his bills; then he would get that pit-boss job and tell me I would never have to hustle again.

I hoped I'd meet a high roller that night so I could show Johnny how connected I was in town, so I could start making my dream come true.

Every day for the next week, sometime between 3 and 4 A.M., I drove to Johnny's place with stacks of hundred-dollar chips and handfuls of bills. I threw them into the air as I walked in the door. We laughed at all the men who gave me so much money. He called them "stupid jerks" as he scooped up my earnings and put then into his dresser drawer. He said he was going to buy me a home on Sunrise Mountain and that I'd be able to get my daughters and have them live with us. I was so happy!

Then he sang to me and played music so we could dance. He ran me a hot bubble bath surrounded by candles and washed and massaged my back and legs as I sipped a drink. Then he prepared a wonderful dinner before we made love. I felt like a queen and I slept secure in his arms.

Johnny was an immaculate housekeeper, and I never had to do any of the work around the place. I never cooked, washed clothes, ironed, or did laundry. Johnny took care of it all. I was his racehorse, and he kept me rested for the next run.

In turn, I pampered him with everything he wanted. I gave him money and he bought custom-made clothes, monogrammed silk shirts, alligator shoes, and leather jackets. He bought a classic white Thunderbird with a hardtop that snapped off, a continental wheel on the back. He said it was for me, but he bought it with my money. He never got that pit-boss job, and the only money he had was mine.

Then he said he wanted to drive me to the casinos and pick me up after work each night. At first I thought it was a great idea, and then I realized he had my car, could do anything he wanted, and keep control of me in that way. When I asked what he did while I was gone, he always said he was looking for work. Then one night, I noticed him following me around in the casinos while I worked. At first I thought it was kind of fun, but later I felt he was stalking me.

Johnny showed up unannounced at the Sands, for example, and watched me from the bar while I sat with Frank and the guys. I never let on that I knew him, and he always kept his distance. If I went upstairs, he waited for me in the bar and gave me a ride home.

I thought that if I could make more money than any woman he had known before me, Johnny would help me fulfill my dreams. In reality, I was giving up my independence, letting him control me and my money. I was in love with him, I thought, but I didn't really know what love was. I'd been heavy into uppers and downers for years. I was only in love with love.

Once after a big night on the town, I came back to my apartment, and Johnny was waiting for me. I opened my purse and poured out all the money I'd made on the table, so he'd see I had a good night.

"Honey, you're just a little moneymaker, aren't you?" Johnny said as he put his arms around me and squeezed me tight.

"I told you I'd do good out there," I smiled.

"Baby, we have enough dough. Let's go to Palm Springs for a week," Johnny suggested.

I had been working seven days a week; I was excited about his idea; so the next day off we went. Johnny checked us into a beautiful place in Palm Springs. It had a Jacuzzi, and we sat in it the first night and drank a bottle of tequila we had picked up along the way. We went to dinner at the best restaurants and shopped in the finest shops, buying things for Johnny, for the girls, and for me. I loved ZhaZha Gabor's shop.

The next day, Johnny called and invited a friend to our digs. Ginger was a tall redhead in her forties, the madam of a brothel in Palm Springs. I'd never met a madam, and it was fun to talk with her. Little did I know that she knew Johnny because he had had two girls working for her.

You see, Johnny was an "old man" or pimp. Pimps found girls who needed money. Usually they were young and homeless; always they were without resources, or thought they were. A pimp said he'd take care of a girl. He'd wine, dine, and show her how to please a man sexually; then he'd place her in a brothel to bring in the cash. A pimp knew the madam would take care of a girl's health and business. She made sure the girl saw a doctor, who gave her penicillin shots to protect against clap and gonorrhea (of course, there are worse things now). The madam provided the girls with johns; her bouncer would not let the girls leave the house.

At the end of each day a madam paid her girls 60 percent for each trick they turned. After a two-week stay, the madam called the pimp to come get his girl—she wanted new girls to keep her tricks interested. The pimp jumped in his new Cadillac, picked up his girl, and took her to another establishment. After about two months switching her from one house to another, he gave her a two-week rest, wining and dining her until she returned to the grindstone.

So the girls moved around, staying two weeks at a brothel at a time, and gave their pimps all their money. A pimp told his girl she was his only squeeze, but most had two or three.

The johns came to the brothel and looked the women over. They chose a girl and paid the madam for fifteen minutes of time. The girl took the trick to a room with a red light over the door, inside and out. When time was up, the bouncer checked on the girl. If the trick wanted more time, he handed over more money or was told to get his pants on. The bouncer took care of the tricks who got out of hand and made sure they paid for what they wanted, so the girls like having them around.

I thought that was a terrible way to live. I felt sorry for the girls who had fallen into that kind of a trap. I didn't see that in a slightly different way I was there too.

At the end of our week in Palm Springs, I felt rested and restored, even more in love with Johnny. Driving back to Vegas, we stopped to get gas and have a drink or two at a nearby bar. Johnny had too much and asked me to drive his Caddie, handing over the keys.

As soon as we got on the highway, he complained about my driving, and he kept it up. Nothing I did was right. Finally, I said, "If you wanted to drive the car, why didn't you do it and leave me alone?

"Pull this damn car over," he said.

We were in the middle of the desert, so it was easy for me to pull over right away; he got out, walked around the car, and opened the door. He grabbed my left arm and yanked me out of the car and down onto the pavement. His eyes were angry.

"Bitch, get around there in the passenger seat and shut up," he yelled. "And don't start bawling, either."

After a moment, he realized what he'd done and reached to pull me from the ground. "Oh, I'm so sorry. I didn't mean to do that, honey."

I didn't know what to think. Suddenly I was afraid; I didn't understand his treating me like that. He didn't say a word the rest of the way back, except that when I cried a little, he asked me please to stop crying. I did, and he said he had lost his manners.

When we got back to my apartment, Johnny was instantly himself again. He opened the car door for me, saying, "Come on, you little love baby. Come on in, and let me wipe your tears."

"Why did you treat me like that?" I asked. I was still hurt, shook up, but I was willing to let him make me feel better.

Johnny took me inside, rolled us a joint, and fixed me a drink. He was very sweet, apologizing again and again for the way he had treated me, blaming it on the drinking. Then he made love to me all night long. Naturally, I forgave him his earlier behavior. It was easy to chalk it up to his drinking.

25

One afternoon I didn't work, and Johnny and I took a drive. We stopped at a bar just outside Palm Springs. He ordered drinks and I made a stop in the rest room. When I came out, a guy walked up, put his arms around me, said I was beautiful, and tried to kiss me. I just pushed him away.

After a few hours of drinking, Johnny decided we better get a motel room, and I grabbed my purse and followed. After I got in the car, I mentioned the incident near the rest room, and Johnny slapped me. He kept on slapping me, harder and harder, and I covered my head with my arms.

"You better stop that, you son of a bitch." I jumped up on the front seat of the convertible.

He stepped on the gas pedal, and I fell into the back seat. Then I jumped out on the trunk because I wanted to get away from him. I thought he would let me off the back of the car, but suddenly he gunned it again. This time I fell to the pavement. I sat there dazed, and he gunned it again, spinning the car to stop in front of me.

"What the f… are you doing? You almost hit me," I screamed.

He got out of the car, walked over, grabbed my head with both of his hands, and slammed it hard on the curb.

"Someone help me!" I screamed. "Please, someone help me!"

A couple of guys came running and asked whether I wanted them to call the cops.

"No, I'll be okay."

But Johnny looked like he was going to kill me. I got up, and he put me in the car and drove to a motel. When he parked the car, I ran into the bar to be away from him. I stayed there until it closed, then snuck into the room. He was out cold, so I went to sleep.

The next day, I had a big knot on my head. It was so sore I thought I was going to have to see a doctor. Instead, I took four pills and went back to sleep for the day. After that, Johnny was nice to me. He brought me flowers, wine, a new bathing suit, candy, and a card that said how much he loved me and how sorry he was. I said I'd leave him if he ever did that again.

Later that week, I got a call to meet Frank Sinatra at the Sands. I didn't tell him, or anyone else, about what Johnny had done, though I know Frank would have stuck up for me. Who knows what he might have done? But I never mixed my personal life with business. None of the girls did that.

Frank, Dean, Sammy, Annette, and I went to see Vic Damone's show at the Flamingo. It had been a long time since I'd seen Vic, and I looked forward to his performance. During the show, Frank, Sammy, and Dean heckled Vic unmercifully from our table, stopping the show several times. They made loud, rude comments and were generally obnoxious. At one point, all three got on the stage and took over the show. Vic calmly went along with the joke, and the audience loved it.

After the show, the five of us went back to the Sands. We were all pretty lit, so Frank, Dean, Sammy, Annette, and I decided to have an early morning snack in the Garden Room, an all-glass-sided coffee shop with a bird's-eye view of the pool and grounds. After the rest of us had ordered, Frank he told the waiter he wanted a rare, regular-sized hamburger.

"Put it on the grill, turn it over, and take it off. Nothing fancy . . . just a regular hamburger."

After what seemed like forever, the waiter placed a hamburger in front of Frank, who put his hands on his hips, looked at the plate, and said, "What the hell is that?" He picked up the bun, looked at the hamburger, about an inch thick and as big around as a saucer, and slammed the bun down on the meat.

"These stupid shits don't even know how to take an order," he yelled. He stood up, kicked over his chair, and grabbed the plate with the hamburger. He stomped to the kitchen, pushed open the swinging door, and threw it at the chef.

"You're fired, you asshole," Frank shouted into the kitchen. Then he came back to the table, cussing up a storm. Everybody in the place could hear him. His bodyguard came to the table to calm him down, but he told him to get out of his face.

"You, bitch, you're fired," he yelled at the waitress, who was still standing at our table, trembling. She started to cry and ran out of the coffee shop, ripping off her apron on the way.

Carl Cohen came in and tried to quiet Frank down, too. But Frank now owned 9 percent of the Sands, and he wanted things his way.

I leaned over and whispered, "Frank, let's get the hell out of this joint. Let's go up to your room and have some fun. That'll calm you down."

"This broad has the right idea," he said, grabbing my arm and pulling me from the chair. Over to his suite we went. Sitting on the couch, we had a drink. He was upset about the waitress and chef, about how they couldn't take a decent order. I took him to the bedroom, hoping to settle him down, and he curled up in my arms. He immediately went to sleep, and I went to my apartment. He had to leave early the next day.

When I got home, Johnny was sitting in the kitchen, drinking and waiting for me: "Where in the hell have you been? How did you do tonight?"

"I had a good night, money-wise," I told him. "But Frank ended up in a bad mood and his bodyguard couldn't settle him down, so I had to take him to his room and calm him down."

"You dumb whore! I saw you out there with him. You were smiling and carrying on like you were having fun. You're not supposed to go out and have a good time with these guys. You're supposed to be working."

"What the hell's wrong with you, Johnny? Why were you following me?" I asked.

"Well, I saw you on Frank's arm, and I saw you laughing and talking to Dean Martin and Sammy Davis Jr. You really pissed me off."

"What's gotten into you? I always smile and look like I'm having fun with my tricks. That's what I'm there for." He was scaring me.

Johnny stood up, walked over, and pushed me onto the couch with one shove.

"You've been out having yourself a good time while I've been sitting in this apartment all night," he said.

"That's your choice," I responded. "You could go out and get a job. Then you wouldn't have to sit in this place."

"You're a big enough job for me to take care of, doing your laundry, cleaning your apartment, taking care of your cars, giving you a massage every night, pampering your young ass all the time."

"You don't have to pamper me any longer." I got up from the couch, ran into the bedroom, and started throwing his clothes from the closet. I had been scared too many times, and I wanted him out of my life.

Johnny came in behind me, spun me around, and began slugging me in the face, arms, and back. I screamed for him to stop, but he pounded harder and harder.

I hit him back and scratched him on the face. He grabbed a hand mirror off the dresser and smashed it against the back of my head. Blood flew everywhere. I fell on the floor, stunned from the blow.

Johnny grabbed my left arm, pulled it straight out and stomped on it as hard as he could. I heard the bone snap as pain shot through my arm. I was screaming, kicking him on his legs, trying for where it would really hurt him. I thought he was going to kill me. I screamed for help, but no one heard me.

Everything stopped for a fraction of a second, then Johnny dropped onto the floor: "Oh, honey, I'm so sorry." He picked me up, put me on the bed, and got a cold towel for my head.

My arm began to swell instantly. It throbbed with pain. I could hardly stand it. Johnny helped me to the car and took me to Sunrise Hospital. I didn't say a word all the way there. In the emergency room, a doctor sewed up my head and set my broken arm. He put the arm in a cast from my shoulder to my wrist. When he asked me what had happened, I told him I had fallen down a flight of stairs. Johnny told me to say that as he drove me over, and I was afraid of what he might do if I did otherwise.

Back at my apartment, Johnny was all love and attention. He cuddled up against me on the bed, trying to make up. He said it would kill him if I left. Still, all I could think of was how to get away from him, but even then I thought I loved him. I thought he had a problem with anger, and that if I didn't make him mad, everything would be okay. He did so much at home for me, and I felt important and needed when I took care of him with my money.

How had we come to this? Was it going to be this way all my life? What had I done to deserve this? Johnny promised and promised he would never attack me again, and I believed him—again. He kept saying he loved me, and I accepted it.

And how could I get out, anyway? Johnny had put everything in his sister's name. Legally, I didn't own a thing!

I was out of circulation for two months—Johnny had made a big mistake, cutting off his generous bread and butter. But I had a little money stashed away, and we were able to live off my savings until I was back on my feet. Johnny made no effort whatsoever to get a job.

After two months in confinement, I told Johnny I wanted a bigger place to live. I went looking for property and soon found a spot on Sunrise Mountain. I bought a half-acre lot, and Johnny convinced me, again, into putting it in his sister's name. "She has a full-time job," he told me, "and what you do isn't legal."

I ordered a double-wide trailer to put on the land. Johnny sold his trailer and moved in with me. The trailer was set up a few weeks later, and it was beautiful! There were three bedrooms, a bath and a half, and a living room and dining room. It even had a sunken tub in the master bedroom.

I hired a contractor to construct a circle drive in front, and gardeners landscaped the rest of the property with shrubs and flowers. I bought a swing set for the girls and furnished the house with French Provincial couches, tables, and lamps. I bought double beds for the girls' bedroom and a new bedroom set for Johnny and me. I figured I was set. I finally had the perfect home for my girls.

Johnny had kept his promise and been so loving to me that I decided to sell my Thunderbird and buy him a XKE Jaguar. I hated to let the T-bird go, but I liked his Caddie better. Then I sent money to my ex, Bob, who had remarried. He put the girls on a plane to Las Vegas, and I picked them up at the airport. My dream was finally coming true. I had my girls, and things were going smoothly with Johnny. I hustled just three days a week, so I could be home most of the time and be a real mother.

Heaven lasted for about eight months; then Johnny started beating me again. He said I was getting lazy and that I should go out more often. I said he should get a job. This time, he blackened my eye. I was afraid the girls would hear us, so I didn't scream when he hit me. Again he apologized and begged me to forgive him. I called Bob and told him I had to send the girls back because Johnny was violent. Bob agreed, so I bought two tickets and sent the girls back to live with him. I didn't want them to see me this way.

After another three-month reprieve, Johnny beat me again. This time he broke my right leg after knocking me to the floor with a punch. He kicked and kicked me until I begged him to stop. Blood was everywhere. I was terrified. The next day, I had a cast on my leg and bruises covering my body.

I took many beatings from Johnny. Once, in Hollywood, he punched me in the face and knocked me out cold. I had been seeing some tricks, and afterwards I picked him up for drinks (I had already been drinking). I got so smashed I drove the wrong way on Santa Monica Boulevard. When we got to our motel he started slapping me, and I slapped him back. I always fought back, and sometimes I landed a good punch or two. But it was no way to live . . . he was a controller and I was the puppet on his string. I couldn't love him into being good.

It took about three months for my broken leg to heal. During that time, I got a lot of calls from my friends on the strip, asking me what was wrong and when I would be back. Finally I told Annette, Audrey, Laurie, and Patsy the truth, but I told the pit bosses and casino owners I'd had an accident and couldn't work.

Patsy said, "Jane, get the hell away from him."

"Patsy, he has all my money—I can't leave him."

"Forget the money, Jane. You can always make more. Get away from him now before he kills you."

I appreciated everyone's concern; I felt better knowing someone cared about me. But what I really needed was to start caring about myself.

26

Johnny and I argued all the time. I went out seven nights a week just to get away from him. One night after an argument, I told him I was going to see my daughters. He didn't say no, didn't put up a fight. He just let me go.

I stayed with Mom and brought the girls to her house. Mom had remarried, and she and her new husband lived in a beautiful home on Sunnycrest Drive in Fullerton Hills, California. Mom and I took the girls to the San Diego Zoo, out to lunch, and shopping. Then I took them back to Bob's house and drove to Hollywood.

I wanted to see Whisky a Go Go, which had opened on Sunset Boulevard in 1964, before returning to Las Vegas. This popular music venue featured go-go girls—dancing in cages suspended from the ceiling—the first thing I saw as I walked through the door. The girls wore fringed mini-dresses and go-go boots and gyrated to the music. I had never been in a place with so many young people.

After a few hours of meeting and talking with new people, I met a guy who was an art director for Warner Brothers. He invited me to his home and gave me directions. After I finished my drink, I drove to the house.

His directions took me into the hills overlooking North Hollywood. After parking the car, I walked to an elevator that took me up to his hilltop home, built around a huge tree growing in the middle of his living room. Too cool! He had drinks ready, we had dinner together, and he phoned a few people asking them to join us.

He handed me a short kimono, and when the other eight people showed up, he gave each of them one, too. We sat around in our robes, naked beneath, having cocktails! Soon, the art director started a reel-to-reel porno movie in the bedroom, the picture as large as the wall. Everyone stood around talking and watching the life-size figures doing their thing. A few drinks later, everyone was licking or sucking everyone else, several at a time.

I remember thinking they must be really bored with life to be doing this for entertainment. Maybe it was the 'Sixties and love, love, love, but it wasn't for me. I told the art director I had to leave. He said to call him the next time I was in town.

A little loaded when I left, I put the top down on the Caddie and headed back to Vegas with the radio booming disco, my hair flying in the wind. I felt like a kid again. When I got home, I told Johnny about the party, and he thought it was really cool.

Not more than a week later, he invited over some new friends—George, who was a pimp, and his "old lady," Margo. After we had few drinks, Margo got down on the floor, took a vibrator out of her purse, and proceeded to enjoy herself in front of us.

"Get it, Margo, get it!" George yelled, encouraging her.

Then Margo crawled over to me and started playing with my legs. She ran the vibrator over her body, then mine. She pulled me to the floor and started to remove my underwear. Johnny was going along with it, turned on, but the whole thing sickened me.

"I just want to party," she said.

I went into the bathroom and cried. Johnny came in, and I asked him what was going on. I didn't understand what he wanted. He begged me to go out and be part of the orgy.

"You really want to see me making love with this woman?"

"You did it for Frank Sinatra. I want you to do it for me."

"I thought we had something more sacred than that," I told him. "It's a job on the strip, not something you do with someone you love, not with people you know."

But Johnny wasn't changing his mind. And I thought, "Oh, what the hell, I'll let Margo do it."

I didn't want to do it, but I would give Johnny what he wanted. He could watch and get horny and screw me, then maybe he'd shut up about it. We'd been together a year—maybe he needed a diversion. But he didn't care about what I wanted, and that made him just like the johns. I felt my love for him melting away. He was just another trick.

I went back to the living room to give Johnny what he wanted. I lay down on the floor, and Margo did her thing—which felt better than anything my old man had done. That was scary! Through it all, Johnny sat on the couch with an erection. When Margo finished, he got on top of me, while George and Margo went at it on the floor next to us.

After the orgy and a few more drinks, George and Margo left. I hated what Johnny had made me do, and I told him how I felt.

"Oh, you liked it. You know you did," he scoffed.

"Yeah, as a matter of fact, she was better than you," I said. But he was too drunk to respond.

Through our remaining time together, John brought women home for sex parties with me. He liked to see two women making love, and I didn't know what to do but go along. I tried to meet his needs, no matter the cost to my self-respect.

About a month after that first "party," I was having a drink at the Dunes with Sid Wyman. He wondered whether I was available to accompany a friend from New York to a dinner show.

"I always have time for your friends, Sid."

He told me to be in the lounge that evening, so he could introduce me to Irving H. He didn't tell me anything else. That's how it went with high rollers. I often knew them only as Mr. L., Mr. P. or just Irving or Sam—no need to know more. Usually, they were married or involved in business and wanted anonymity. I respected their wishes then.

Irving turned out to be a Jewish man in his fifties, of medium height and build, a fun-loving guy who seemed to have tons of money. He wanted to see *Folies Bergère* at the Tropicana, so we took a cab to the hotel. On the way through the casino to the dinner show, we ran into my friend Ben Jaffe, one of the bosses in town. I hadn't seen him for awhile and he invited us to have dinner on the house. All I had to do was sign my name. Things were different then.

After dinner and seeing the show, we hit the crap tables on the way out. I thought it would be fun to see the Mary Kay Trio at the Last Frontier (later the Frontier). Irv was willing, so we grabbed another cab.

We enjoyed the lounge show, one of the best in town, and all in all we had a wonderful time, despite our business relationship. Irving was a gentleman, and he said I was just what he needed in his life. We went back to the Dunes, I took him around the world, and he asked whether I'd ever been to New York. I hadn't, so he told me about it. I said it would be fun to visit him there.

"I'll call you next week and set something up."

"You be sure to do that." I could see he was attracted to me and that he might be a good catch. His gift to me had been very generous!

When I got home, I told Johnny about Irving, that he might want me to come to New York for a price.

"Are you sure you want to do that?"

"For a price, I'll do anything." Maybe this was my chance to leave Johnny behind.

The next afternoon, Annette phoned, asking me to meet her and a friend of one of her johns (for a trick). "Do you know Howard Hughes is staying here at the Desert Inn?" she asked after we met in the lounge.

"You've got to be kidding! That old duffer?" I said.

"Let's go to his room. I bet we could make a ton of money."

We'd both had enough liquor to try anything, and we took the elevator to the floor where he was staying. Two guards stopped us before we exited the elevator. Howard had taken up the whole floor—I thought that was weird.

"You girls get back downstairs," a guard said. "You don't belong here."

"You tell Howard that Janie and Annette are here."

"Does he know you?"

"No, but he will when we get through," I giggled.

Little did we know Hughes was there to buy up most of Vegas! He did and was the cause of subsequent changes in the city—in with the calculating corporations, out with the personal welcome and warmth.

Two weeks later, I received two dozen, long-stemmed, red roses with a card signed, "Love, from your Secret Admirer." I had no idea who had sent them, but later that day I got a call from Irving.

"Did you get your flowers?"

"I sure did. Thanks for telling me who they were from."

"I picked up a little piece of jewelry I thought you would just love. It should be there tomorrow," Irving said. "Can you come to New York?"

"Well, yes, I can. I'd love to come. But there are so many things I should take care of before I leave."

"How much money do you need to take care of them?"

I named a rather large sum, and he sent it the next week. Along with the money came an airline ticket to New York City, and a 14-karat-gold bracelet with a cluster of diamonds that flips up to show the time. Johnny drove me to the airport, and off I went to New York.

Irving was at the gate to greet me. We walked through the New York terminal and into a big white limousine. Irving took me to a hotel right off Park Avenue. My suite was luscious! Two powder-blue loveseats faced each other in the large, immaculate, living room. There was another seating area by the window, affording a view of Central Park. The king-sized bed in the other room was dressed in a pink-and-blue satin comforter. The drapes and accessories were perfectly coordinated. If Irving was trying to impress me, he was doing a good job of it.

He had said he would give me time to unpack and freshen up before he picked me up for dinner. That evening I couldn't help looking up at the skyscrapers on the way to the restaurant. New York was so exciting!

"You know I'm a married man," Irving told me later at the hotel. "But my home is quite a way out, in the Gold Coast [New Jersey] area, so there's really nothing to worry about. My wife and I don't get along that well, and we haven't for years."

Irving said he would take me shopping the next day, that I would love the shops in New York City because they had everything—the city was the center of high fashion. When he left that night, I stood at the window and wondered what all the other people in New York were doing. Here I was in the middle of Manhattan with a man, probably worth millions, who seemed to care about me. And he hadn't even asked for sex. I could get used to this!

When Irving invited me to New York, I thought it was for a week, but one turned into two, and two into three. Finally, he said he wanted to keep me—he didn't want me to leave. With his lavish gifts and pocketfuls of money, I had no reason to go back to Johnny, with his weird sexual needs and his violence. I still sent him a weekly check to cover his expenses, but he had no control of me here.

One evening, as Irving and I were having dinner, I told him about my daughters. When I became somewhat emotional, he said, "Well, honey, if that's all that's bothering you, let's have them sent out here."

That was such a nice thing for him to do, I started to cry. I grabbed him, kissed him, thanked him, and asked him when.

"As soon as you can make arrangements, I'll get your tickets."

That evening we went back to the hotel, and I took him around the world—the first time since I'd come to New York.

I phoned Bob the next morning and asked him to send the girls to New York for three weeks. He thought it was a great idea and agreed to take them to the airport. The girls were old enough to fly alone, and school had just ended.

Irving took me to the airport in his Cadillac to pick up the girls. The stewardess brought them off the plane and checked my ID. We hugged and kissed, and cried before I introduced them to Irving. He said they were beautiful.

Cindy and Roberta were excited when they saw the hotel suite, but Irving had something else in mind: "I have a surprise for you girls. I'm going to take you up to the Catskill Mountains, where it's cool." He told us how beautiful it was there, how much we would enjoy it. There were all kinds of activities for children. He would check us into a hotel and we could be together, alone, for the whole time.

Realizing I would be the only adult there with the kids, I asked Irving whether he might bring my friend Carol and her son to join us.

"No problem, Janie, if that will make you happy."

Carol and her son, Charlie, flew out three days later. We picked them up in the limousine. Carol was impressed.

"Janie! Where did you meet this one?"

"I have myself a real nice one this time, don't I?"

"You could get really spoiled this way, couldn't you?"

"Honey, I'm already spoiled."

We were off to the Catskills with Irving. We rode in the white leather seats in the back, sipping cocktails, while Cindy (nine), Roberta (seven), and Charlie (eight) sipped on sodas, ate chips, and looked at the landscape. We drove into the grand entry of Green Acres late in the afternoon. Irving had made arrangements for us to stay in a private cabin.

We spent three glorious weeks in the Catskills, basking in the sun, waited on hand and foot. The girls and Charlie took part in the children's activities, and I loved being with my best friend. We returned for another day together in New York; then Irving sent our four guests back to California. That night, I told him how much I appreciated what he had done and that I would always love him for that.

He told me he loved me too, but I knew we had no future. Irving was a married man and forty years older to boot.

27

As the months went by, I started to catch Irving in little lies. For instance, he called me from the car phone, saying he'd be at the suite in a couple of hours, and the next minute he'd open the door. He didn't want me to go out with anyone but to wait for him, be ready when he wanted me.

Another time, he said he was having two bicycles sent to my daughters. I told Cindy and Roberta that the bikes were coming, then found out he'd never sent them. When I first got to New York, he bought me a big diamond ring. But it wasn't really mine. He insisted I wear it every time we went out—he liked to show me off.

This kind of stuff went on all the time. When I asked him why he lied, he brushed me off. I soon saw he wanted to control everything I did. My world was very small; I certainly had no friends. I was learning what it meant to be a "kept" woman, and I wanted out.

One evening Irving and I met another couple in a cocktail lounge for drinks before dinner. The gentleman was in his fifties and the beautiful young woman about twenty-five years old. In the rest room, we talked. She told me that her parents had promised her to him as soon as she turned eighteen. It was a tradition between their families—they would soon be married.

I couldn't believe it. How could they arrange something like this from birth? It was the 1960s! And I could tell she thought it was her obligation to fulfill their demands. I wondered how many other girls in America went through this. It was a whole new world.

One day when I was tired of Irving and his games, I pretended I had a headache so he would go home. After he left, I slipped out and took a taxi to Jilly's on Broadway, a club owned by Jilly Rizzo, Sinatra's friend. I thought Jilly or Honey might be there. While I at the club, Johnny Carson walked in. He was more handsome than he appeared on television. I think he was doing *The Tonight Show* from New York at that time.

Sitting next to me at the bar was a young woman in her early twenties. We got to talking, and she told me her name was Sheri. About an hour later, she asked whether I'd like to go to a place that was young and fun. I said I needed some fun, and we headed for a cab to Greenwich Village. Sheri lit up a joint on the way. She said I had probably never been to a place like the one where we were going, but that I would enjoy it.

I thought, "My God! Here I am in my diamonds and furs, smoking pot, driving down crazy New York streets with a strange woman, going to some bar I've never been to before. Have I lost my mind, or am I just in need of a good time?"

I got a little nervous when I saw how seedy the neighborhood was, but then cab dropped us off, and we went into the joint. There was a long bar along the front, with booths and a dance floor in the back. It was packed. We went to the bar and ordered drinks, and I started to look around. It took me about ten minutes to realize where I was.

"Are these all girls in here? Some of them look like guys."

"They sure do, and they're a hell of a lot of fun," Sheri said.

"Is this a queer bar?"

"Yes, it is."

"God, Irving will kill me if he found out."

"Nobody's going to bother you. They can tell by looking at you that you're straight."

Well, I was here, so I decided to settle in and have fun. I was high, but I could see that no one was going to tear my clothes off and have her way with me. (Besides, I'd already done that with Johnny and his friends.)

Sheri introduced me to a few of her friends, then took me into the back room. We found a booth and watched the girls dance. Some of the women who looked like men were really cute. My curiosity was aroused.

Soon we had seven girls sitting at our table. One was pursued by several of the more feminine girls, who wanted to dance. She was a cute little thing with a man's haircut, shorter than me. She ignored the rest of the girls, looked right into my eyes, and said, "I'm going to have you."

"Sure you are, honey!" I thought it was a big joke. She kept looking at me, every once in awhile coming over to chat.

I was having a great time, enjoying my night out, and I couldn't believe it when the time came for closing. One girl invited me to her house. She said we'd smoke some pot and drink a little. Here was my chance to party! These women were my age, and I was having fun. I didn't care about their lifestyle. What went on behind closed doors was their business.

Ten of us went to the apartment nearby. I couldn't believe how relaxed I felt there. It was nice not to have a man looking or wanting to touch me. Early in the morning, Sheri dropped me back at the hotel. She gave me her number. I told her that when I got rid of the old man, I'd call.

Soon after that, Irving asked me to accompany him on a business trip to Philadelphia. Just before the plane landed on our return flight, he said that if I saw a short woman walk up to him, I should walk ahead of him so that she wouldn't see me. Sure enough, just as we got off the plane, a short, gray-haired woman walked out of the crowd and slapped him across the face.

"You son-of-a-bitch, I know you're seeing another woman. Is she on this plane with you?"

"You crazy old woman! No!" Irving walked right by her, and she ran after him. She got into the limousine with him, still screaming.

I continued to walk away, and then I realized I had no money. I stopped a complete stranger and asked him for a dime to call the hotel and leave a message at the desk. Suddenly I heard my name paged. It was Irving. He told me to get in a cab and come straight to the hotel. I did what he said, and he was there when I pulled up.

"Jesus Christ, Irving, what are you trying to pull on me?"

"My wife is checking on me, and we're going to have to move you. Pack your things, and I'll have the driver pick up your bags."

I packed my things in a hurry, and the driver picked them up. Off to another hotel we went, Irving and I in his Cadillac. Soon I was in my new suite, more gorgeous than the last. I felt sure Irving's wife was at the suite I'd just abandoned. What wealth this man must have!

Irving showed up later that night, saying everything would be okay. He had spent the afternoon with his wife at the other suite, having lunch, calming her down to get her off his trail. He said she had gotten ahold of his expense report because she wanted to know where he was spending his money. He was trying to convince her he had been alone in the suite for a year, entertaining business guests. I really couldn't blame his wife for being upset about her husband fooling around behind her back. I had been there too.

Then Irving called and said he'd be gone for a couple of days and he'd send one of his boys with an envelope of money for me. Each day, a buffed, well-dressed man personally delivered an envelope filled with cash. After I opened it and removed the money, the man took the envelope, tore it up, burned it in the bathroom sink, and flushed the ashes down the toilet.

"Boy, that's really cops and robbers stuff," I said.

"That's right. You don't know who you're really dealing with, kid." I had no idea what he meant.

My next instruction was to take a cab to meet Irving for dinner at a restaurant downtown. He told me to watch my back. I didn't see anyone on the way over, so I thought everything was okay. I didn't know who I was looking for, but I guessed it was his wife.

When I met Irving at the restaurant, we went into the bar and had a drink. I asked him what was going on. In the past, he said, his wife had hired a private detective to keep him from being with other women.

"Maybe I should go back to Vegas."

"Oh, no, baby, I want you to stay here with me. You make me happier than I've been in a long time."

"Well, if you say it's going to be okay, I'll stay. I don't want to get into any trouble over this." I had confidence he knew what he was doing, and I sat back and relaxed.

Minutes later, some of Irving's friends arrived to join us for dinner. He introduced me to a Mr. Wurlitzer and his girlfriend, a real knock-out, flirty with the men in the restaurant. Irving called him "the juke-box king." Another gentleman, an Italian-looking, older man, joined us after dinner. I saw a gun in a holster under his suit coat when he leaned across the table. Irving had a lot of suspicious-looking characters around him all the time. I never asked questions.

That same night, I called Sheri. Irving had gotten drunk at the restaurant and hit his head on a mirror while bending over to pick up his hat. He had gone home to nurse his headache. The night was still young, I had taken a diet pill, and I was ready to have some fun. Sheri said she would meet me at that same bar in Greenwich Village.

I grabbed a cab and headed out. Sheri and I had a drink, then went out to have a joint in the alley. The girl who had flirted with me went out with us. She introduced herself as Sunny. She seemed like a person I could be friends with.

After the bar closed, Sunny asked a group to her house to party. There she introduced me to Tuinals, a sleeping-pill-type drug, a downer. When I took a Tuinal with coffee, I got really high, keyed up. Once, I took too many and passed out face down in a Greenwich Village bar. My friends poured milk down my throat to revive me. I was glad to have them as my friends because Irving and his wife were becoming a nightmare. Tuinals helped me manage my anxiety.

Irving's wife, I found out, had called my mother in California. How she knew where Mom lived or got her phone number I do not know. Mrs. H. asked her if she knew what I was doing in New York. Mom said that she had no idea why I was there or who I was with but that I was old enough to know what I was doing. Mrs. H. said I'd better watch myself because "Mr. Cosa Nostra's wife" was watching.

Mom immediately called to ask what was going on. She said it sounded like mobsters were after me, and I better get the hell out of there. The call worried me. I had never heard reference to the Cosa Nostra; even then I thought it was just a nickname for Irving, who hadn't revealed anything about his life or his business.

Then Irving told me he was going to have to move me again, that he thought my suite was tapped, and someone was listening to our conversations. He moved me to another hotel the next day, this one with a swimming pool; I used it once in awhile to get some exercise. Otherwise I was a nervous wreck.

I liked the gay people because they were soft and gentle and told it like it was. None of them ever tried to get in my pants. I realized that many people saw my lesbian friends as degenerates and lowlifes, but my perception was that they had broken from the run-of-the-mill, stereotypical, heterosexual lifestyle. It didn't seem to me that men and women got along that well anyway. Every man I knew seemed to want a little chick on the side while his wife stayed home and took care of the house. That seemed a lot sleazier than the life these people led. At least they were honest with themselves and up-front with each other.

Caught between two worlds, literally hiding from investigators in one and keeping my new friends secret from Irving, made me feel I was beginning to crack. I become paranoid, aware of every head that turned towards me, afraid people knew I was "kept." I was used to people looking at me in Vegas, but this made me feel clammy and nauseated. I thought Irving's wife had the mob after me. I worried about whether my daughters would be okay if something happened to me. Finally I went off the deep end.

One day while Irving and I were having lunch in a restaurant, I cried uncontrollably. "Get me out of here! Get me out of here! I can't stand all these people staring at me."

He grabbed my arm, put his arm around me, and hustled me to the door. Now they really were staring. Irving took me to an emergency room, and I told the doctor I couldn't stop crying, that all I could think about were all the tragic things that had happened in my life. I said I just wanted to be locked up in a room where I didn't have to think or worry about anyone.

I was admitted to the hospital, and the doctor told Irving I was having a nervous breakdown. He said I needed to get off the drinking and the drugs, and that I needed some time to think things out. Irving got me a private hospital room that was more like a suite. I spent five days there without any phone calls or visitors. The doctor medicated me to withdraw me from the drugs. A psychiatrist helped me understand my problems and advised me to get help after I left the hospital.

The stay in the hospital was a welcome break. I got a chance to think about my life with Irving and his wife, Johnny and my daughters. I decided I was sick of being told what to do and of being used. I wanted to start a new life. I wanted to get out of prostitution and off drugs. I wanted to meet new friends, have a real job, and be free.

I didn't want to be a toy for men any longer. I was tired of Irving's games and of his wife. I was sick of having to answer to Johnny. Finally, I was tired of being without my girls.

For the next three months, every time I was rid of Irving, I went to the Greenwich Village bar. I made all kind of friends my age, but I continued on the sleeping and diet pills. I was high as hell or docile as a rag doll. One night at a friend's house after sleeping pills and coffee, I felt a warm feeling come over me. Then I felt faint and collapsed. My friends led me to the bedroom to sleep it off.

When I woke the next afternoon, I went back to Irving; he had left a message for me at the desk. He wanted me to go out to dinner, then to the suite for a roll in the hay. I played the part and went to dinner, but halfway through the meal I told him I had a splitting headache. He took me back to the hotel, and as soon as he drove away, I grabbed a cab for Greenwich Village.

Soon after that, I told my mom that I was hanging around some new friends and having a good time.

"Oh, thank God! Maybe now you won't be getting the shit beat out of you by that damned Johnny," she said. "Maybe you won't have to cater to all those old men anymore." She had known what was going on in my life for years, but she hadn't seemed to care.

We had a nice conversation. I told her how I was going to get a place of my own and get a job in New York. She was happy for me. After we talked, I hurried to get dressed. Irving was due to pick me up, and I wanted to be ready. I had to keep him happy until I found a new career.

When Irving arrived, he said we had to sit down and talk.

"What's the matter?"

"Jane, I've been having my men follow you, and they reported that you went to a queer bar in Greenwich Village after I dropped you off the other night. They told me that you've been partying with a bunch of dykes and that after the bar closes, you go with them to an apartment. You know you could be called a queer by associating with that kind of people. I think it's best you take your ass back to Vegas." Irving said. "You're a sick little bitch!" And he slapped me across the face.

I stood up: "You're not going to slap me around, you old fart!" Then I slapped him.

Irving was silent. He just sat there, glaring.

"What have you been doing, having somebody follow me?"

"That's right. I've been doing it for a long time. I have connections. I can find out anything I want about anybody, at any time."

"Jesus Christ! Are you some kind of mobster?" I was getting scared. I didn't know what to expect. I was beginning to realize he was a powerful man. I was even afraid he might have me killed.

"Don't worry about it, bitch."

"Just because I want to have some fun and be around people my own age doesn't mean I'm queer. I'm sick of you old men telling me what to do. Nine months I've spent waiting for you and servicing your every need. I've been good to you. And I've had to put up with your wife having me followed too!"

Irving turned and walked out the door and into the hallway. I heard him knock on the door of the suite next to mine. In a minute, he and a man in a black suit came back in. Irving was carrying a briefcase, and he put it down on the table. It was a tape recorder. He pushed a button, and I heard my conversations with my girlfriends and my mother.

I thought, "My God, I'm going to end up in the river. This guy really is a mobster."

"Now, explain that, you stupid bitch."

"If you'll just listen, I will explain it," I said. I knew I had to convince him that I cared for him and would never hurt him. "Just let me tell you my side of it."

"All right, I'm listening." Irving's face was dark and mean. He stood looking at me, his arms crossed. The man in the black suit stood by the door.

"I got conned into this hustling life because I wanted to get my children back. I'm really a good person. Maybe I take too many pills, but you coerced me into coming to New York. Your wife called my mother and threatened her. You lie to me all the time. I've had a nervous breakdown over all the shit you've put me through. I had no friends here in New York, and I just happen to have become friends with some gay people, who listen to me and understand. They accept me for who I am, and I feel comfortable around them because they don't try to take me to bed."

Irving didn't say a word as I paced the room. I continued: "You're problem is that you hate gay people, and I see them as my new friends. I know you can be understanding when you want to be. I feel you have used me to fulfill your needs. I do like you and hope we can end this by being friends. I don't want to ruin the nine months we've had together. You knew I was a call girl when you met me, and you knew our relationship couldn't possibly last forever. You're still married, and it's not fair that you're cheating. And I can't live like a pet in a cage anymore."

Irving grabbed his hat and overcoat and walked out the door without a word.

As soon as I could, I grabbed a cab to Greenwich Village. Irving hadn't killed me yet, and I didn't care if anyone followed me. When I got there, the bartender bought me a drink and listened to my story. A friend came over and said I could move in with her and her girlfriend. I spent the night with them and went back to the suite the next morning to pack.

About noon, there was a loud knock on the door. I opened it, and there was a man standing in the hallway. He had on a black suit and his eyes sent chills up my spine.

"Jane, Irving sent me with a message. The message is 'Jane, it was nice knowing you. My advice is to go back to Las Vegas.'"

Then he opened his jacket, revealing a shoulder holster with a huge, black gun. He said, "My advice is to get out of town and not to pursue Irving. Never call him, never see him, never talk to him, and don't ever cause him any trouble, or you'll have to answer to me!"

"Yes sir, I understand. I'm leaving today." I couldn't pack fast enough. I was happy to be alive.

I moved in with my friends, not wanting to return to Vegas or Johnny. I had saved some money, and I knew I'd find a job somewhere soon.

28

The next day, I called Johnny and told him that my dealings with Irving were over. Johnny was sweet on the phone. I told him I was going to stay with my gay friends in Greenwich Village until I found my own apartment. He sounded understanding, asking for the address so he could send flowers. He would wait for me to call.

Three days later, Johnny showed up on the doorstep. He had driven the Jaguar across country without stopping to sleep. He said he couldn't wait to see me and wanted to take me back home.

"But, Johnny, you don't understand. I don't want to come back. I've met these really nice girls, and I like being around them. I don't want to turn tricks. I want you to sell my stuff and give me back my money."

"Oh, honey, you're just going through a phase. You've been through a lot of shit since you've been with Irving, and you think these gay girls are your good friends, but they're not. You're just overwhelmed with everything, and now you're infatuated with these queer people.

Hell, I know you're not gay! You don't just turn gay overnight."

"Johnny, I'm sick and tired. I'm sick of you taking all my money. I'm tired of being beaten up, and I don't want anything to do with you and your crazy sex parties. I hate it, and I hate you for doing that to me."

Johnny didn't say a word. He knew not to push. For two days, he sweet-talked me, letting me think he was going to give back my money, and if I wanted, sell everything and buy something in New York. He said whatever I wanted was fine with him, that he didn't care where he lived as long as he was with me. He was getting to me.

But when he saw I was not going to change my mind and go with him, Johnny's real self surfaced: "You know, Jane, you're going to have to get your shit together. You don't belong here with these gay people. You belong with me in your home in Vegas."

"I'm so mixed up, Johnny. I don't know what I want to do."

"Well, I guess I just have to throw acid in your friends' faces! That should change your mind about being with your damn gay friends. Hell, I might as well just take your ass down to the river right now and dump you in. You know I'll do it if that's what it comes to, if you don't come back with me. And I will tell your kids you're here with a bunch of queers!"

I was sure he would carry out his threats as he had before: "Okay, okay, Johnny, don't say more. I'm packing my clothes and coming home with you." I cried while writing a note to my friends. I told them how important their friendship was to me and promised to stay in touch with them, hoping they'd understand. Then Johnny grabbed my bags and we left.

Johnny was telling me I needed him to keep me off the downers and get me strong again. *He* needed to get me under control to make money to pay for all my expenses. He said my cheeks were sunken and I was just skin and bones. He said he'd take care of me, preaching all the way back to Vegas, persuading me that I belonged with him.

I went to work on the strip seven days a week, trying to stay away from the house and Johnny. During the several weeks after I returned he just bided his time, trying to keep me happy until he came up with his next surprise. He bought me a ring or something beautiful (I can't remember exactly what, as he did this so many times), and he asked for a new car. I traded the Jaguar for a Corvette Stingray because he'd always hinted that he would love to have one.

One morning when I came home after working all night, he showed me a new Harley Davidson that he'd bought with my money. It was all tricked out in chrome and leather, with side bags, black leather pants, and jacket to match. I think he wanted to show his friends that his woman had a lot of money to buy him toys. George was sporting a new Mercedes Sportster, paid for by Margo, of course.

Then Johnny decided to take flying lessons because George had a new Cessna 300. Johnny started working on me to buy him a plane, too. Then he wanted me to marry him. Again and again he promised to get a job and support me for the rest of my life. But I was still into the drugs, and he knew how to say the things I wanted to hear: "You'll never have to turn another trick, and your girls could come and live with us."

On December 19, 1965, I married Johnny at the Little Chapel in Las Vegas. I was twenty-four years old, and he was forty-five. We took a trip to Arizona for our honeymoon, and when we returned he said he tried to get a job, but he never did. He asked me to help out a little more and turn a few tricks until he found work. I knew he'd lied again. He was conning me the whole time.

I was in a bad spot and couldn't get out. I'd been making so much money and there'd been so much spending that if I didn't work, everything would go to the dogs. Bills were due—I had to go back out on the strip. I was hooked on the money, and I was a fool to give it to Johnny.

During this time I saw Frank Sinatra, after he had married Mia

Farrow in July 1966. Their romance was quite an "item." I certainly was surprised to hear of his marriage on the news. A few weeks later I ran into him in the cocktail lounge at the Sands. He motioned me over for a drink. Sitting at the table with him was a twig of a woman, very young. Frank introduced us, and she seemed to look right through me.

"I heard you got married. Congratulations!" I said. Then I sat and talked with Dean and Sammy, staying away from Frank, not wanting to intrude.

While I was sitting there, I overheard Mia talking to Frank: "Fuck you. I want to go down the street to that disco, you fucking old man." She had little respect; I couldn't believe Frank let her talk to him that way. Mia stormed out of the lounge, apparently headed for the disco.

Frank walked out to the pit to talk to someone, and when he came back, I walked up to him, put both hands on his shoulders, and pushed him against the wall: "Frank, what possessed you to marry that girl? Were you that damn lonely? I thought you liked a woman with a body?"

Frank just stood there. "I don't know why. I just feel like I love her. I don't know what happened. But she's usually pretty sweet," he replied.

"She talks to you like you're dirt under her feet."

"Well, I'm in it now. I don't know how long it's going to last."

I told Frank I was leaving for Los Angeles to see my daughters the next day, that I was concerned for him and hoped he would be happy. I gave him a peck on the cheek and said I'd see him the next time he was in town.

The next time Frank was in Vegas was about a year later. Mia had gone off to shoot a movie, and Frank didn't want her to go. Apparently, this had caused a big fight; they were having serious problems, and it was not long before their divorce.

At the time I heard he was in a party mood, gambling heavily, into

235

the casino for ten to twenty thousand, not that unusual for him. Frank asked Carl Cohen, in the Garden Room, for another marker, and Carl said he wanted him to take care of what he owed first. Frank was enraged and pushed the table over onto Carl. Then he got a golf cart and drove it through a window. Supposedly, Carl slugged him, knocking out two of Frank's teeth. He told Frank he would have to leave the hotel immediately.

I'm glad I wasn't there for that scene. I loved both men and hated even hearing that they got into it that way. I didn't see Frank there again.

Caesars Palace opened August 1966, and a bunch of us, including the bartenders and waiters from one of the bars on the strip, decided to turn the fountains in front of the hotel into the largest bubble bath in Vegas. We parked our cars off Las Vegas Boulevard and, one at a time, walked nonchalantly to the fountains with a box of Mr. Bubble and dumped it in. We were careful to keep our backs to the entrance so no one could see.

Afterwards, we sat in the bar across the street and watched the bubbles overflow. It was one of the funniest things I'd seen. The police came into the bar and asked whether we'd seen anyone near the fountain. No one said a peep. After the police left the bar, we partied 'til the sun came up.

On one of my rounds, I met a singer in the lounge at Caesars Palace. Betty, a waiter, introduced her to me after she had finished her act. Anne, from Ireland, was a brilliant singer in her early twenties. After we had a drink, Anne asked me to drive her to her motel so she could change her clothes.

I took Anne to the motel and waited for her while she showered. When she came out, she was wearing blue jeans, a tucked-in, checked shirt, and a leather belt with a large silver buckle. I sat there in my evening gown and wondered, "Is she gay?"

Anne wanted to drink at a bar down the street from the motel.

When we got there, she found a place there were seats for only two people. I tried to be nonchalant as we made small talk. She, on the other hand, stared at me, making me uncomfortable. She seemed to be flirting with me, but I thought it might be just in my mind.

We spent three hours there, talking about life in general. I thought she was intriguing; I enjoyed her company just as I had enjoyed the girls in New York. Afterwards, I dropped her at her place and went home.

The whole next day, I kept thinking about Anne, alternately talking to myself, saying, "Janie, stop it! Straighten up!" But I kept thinking about the way she looked at me and how talented and nice she was.

That evening, I went to the Sands, turned a few tricks, then went to Caesars Palace to catch Anne's act in the lounge. She asked me to drive her to her motel again, so she could change and get something to eat. This time, when she came out in her jeans and shirt her hair was slicked back like a guy. Sexy!

She must have caught the vibe because she walked over, reached down, took my hand, pulled me up, and kissed me on the lips. I was a bowl of jelly! I felt butterflies in my stomach. This went on for a few weeks. Every time we were together, she kissed me, looking in my eyes, never anything else. But she was making me crazy for her.

One night while we were having drinks at the Red Barn, one of the three gay bars in Vegas then, I confessed to Anne that I had an old man. I told her I didn't know how to get away from him and asked her what I should do.

She said, "You know, I do have very strong feelings for you, but I've known all this time that you're with a man. I don't want to disrupt your life."

"You're not going to mess up my life. I'm just about the most unhappy woman you've ever met." I told her about Johnny and how he beat me, used me, and managed to get all my money.

I drove Anne back to the motel. We sat on the side of the bed and kissed and caressed one another. She undressed me, and we made love. It was heavenly. I was in the arms of a woman, feeling like a whole woman again. We talked for hours, and I was so happy to be with her. She said she was glad she had held back all those weeks.

"I think you should get away from Johnny," Anne said.

"I'm going to. I want to pack my things and get away, but I have to be careful because he might kill me before I get out the door."

Anne rented an apartment the next week and I sneaked over to see her every chance I could.

As time passed, Johnny noticed there was less money. He got suspicious and asked, "What's happening on the strip? How come you're not bringing home as much as you used to?"

"Things are real slow."

"Janie, tell me the truth. What's going on?"

"Nothing's going on. Nothing's changed. I just haven't been lucky lately."

I realized I was living two lives. I wanted to end that, to stop turning tricks. Every day, I did battle inside, keeping up the front of my "straight" life while I spent as much time as I could with the woman I loved.

Anne was with me one day when I was shopping in a hotel dress shop. I wanted her to tell me which of three dresses I had tried on was the most attractive. When I walked out in the third dress, there was Johnny, standing next to Anne.

"It looks like you're having yourself a fun afternoon," Johnny snarled. "Who's this? Your friend, I suppose."

"Yes, she's a friend of mine. She's a singer at Caesars Palace lounge. Her name is Anne."

"Jane, get your shit and get your ass home." He looked ready to kill me.

"I'm not coming home."

"Get home now, if you know what's good for you." He turned and walked out the door.

I had parked the Cadillac right outside the dress shop. Johnny probably spotted it as he was driving by. Anne and I got in and drove to her apartment. She told me everything would be okay, but I was really worried.

That evening, I called Johnny and told him I would pick up my clothes the next day. I said I wouldn't be with him again, that he could have everything. All I wanted was my freedom.

"You stupid bitch! You're going to end up with nothing. You're going to end up like all the queers, on the streets. You'll be sorry," he yelled through the phone.

"I'm getting my clothes, I'm leaving you, and I'm never going to turn another trick. It's over!"

Afterwards, Anne suggested we have a few drinks to settle me down. We drove to the Red Barn and were playing the slots when a girl came running in.

"Somebody has set fire to a big pile of clothes in the parking lot!"

Anne and I ran out to see. There in the parking lot was a pile of ripped-up dresses, evening dresses, and mink stoles—mine. Johnny had torn up all the pictures of me with Frank Sinatra and other celebrities, thrown them on top of the clothes, and set the pile on fire. I tried to run over and put it out, but it was too late to save anything.

I heard a car peel out from the boulevard, and I looked up to see Johnny in the Corvette. He was parked across the street watching to see what I'd do.

I stood in the parking lot and screamed, "No . . . No . . . No!"

Five guys came running from the bar to protect me, pulling me back into the bar. Anne held me and tried to get me to stop crying.

"They're only material things. At least you have your life. You can buy new clothes again. It's a good thing that you're getting away from him, Janie."

I didn't think I'd ever get over it—burning my clothes, which I had depended on to make a living, seemed like the worst thing he could do. The people in the bar bought me drinks to cheer me up, and after awhile I started to feel a little better. But I was scared, and I never went back to my mobile home. I began to hope it was over for good.

Some of Anne's friends had invited us to meet them at Maxine's, out on Tonapah Highway (now Rancho Drive). I drove into the pitch-black desert with the top of the Caddie down. We were alone on the two-lane highway. Cruising at fifty-five miles per hour, I saw a pair of headlights coming toward us. When the car got closer, I could see it was George in his convertible. Johnny was sitting on the back of the passenger seat, waving something.

Suddenly, I could hear pop . . . pop . . . pop. As George approached, I saw Johnny waving a handgun, shooting at me as they sped by. I ducked when I saw the barrel pointed at my face and floored it.

"Get down, damn it. Hide your head, and get down on the floor. That son-of-a-bitch is shooting at us. He's crazy!"

The bullets whizzed by as I pushed the speed to 120, trying to avoid the fire. When I looked into my rear-view mirror, I saw they'd made a U-turn and were after me.

I skidded into Maxine's graveled parking lot, the car doing a spin before landing snug at the front door. We jumped from the car (I didn't even turn it off), and as I opened the door I heard gunshots as George and Johnny flew by. I screamed at the bartender, "Call the police. My old man is trying to kill me!"

I had never been so scared. We ran to the rest room to hide, huddling in the small stall, shaking until the police arrived.

The officers took a report, listening to my story but not seeming to care. In their eyes I was a queer, and from their remarks I could tell they hated queers.

The cops examined my car and said there were no bullet holes to prove a shooting. The popping sounds had probably come from backfiring. With that, they left, and Johnny and George got away with what they had done. After that Johnny stalked and harassed me daily. My confidence dwindled, and I began to feel paranoid again.

The next week, Anne and I and some friends were at the Red Barn —the only place in town we could be ourselves. We were sitting at the bar when we heard a crash at the front. Everybody ran outside to see what had happened. The awning and its wooden posts had fallen onto the hood of my car.

We all saw Johnny drive away in the Corvette. He had used the set of keys he had for the Cadillac and driven it into the bar. The car was only scratched, but I offered to pay for the awning, and I did.

After this incident, I called Johnny to say that if he didn't stop harassing me, I would have him arrested. He told me he was sorry, that he was crazy over losing me. He said I was killing him slowly and begged me to come back.

"I hope you do die for all the things you've done. Now, you've tried to kill me three times. You'll never have another chance. You're out of my life forever."

That was the last time I talked to him. I called a cab for the airport and bought a ticket for California. Crossing the tarmac to board the plane, I thought I saw him coming after me.

I ran for my life.

Epilogue & Resources

After leaving Las Vegas, I stayed with my mother for a time. I got a job as a nurse's aide, and occasionally had my daughters overnight. I talked with Anne on the phone but did not see her again. I went through a series of jobs including prostitution, a series of lesbian partners and cities, and an attempt at suicide. Finally I got work that led to becoming a quality-control technician for the manufacture of circuit boards, only to become the victim of a disabling industrial accident. All that and what follows is really another story.

Ten years after I left Vegas, I noticed some bumps on my breasts. A surgeon scooped raw silicone from my body for seven hours, implanted two bags filled with liquid silicone and sewed me up. That resulted in gangrene and the removal of both breasts. Silicone, still floating in my body, could block an artery to heart or lungs and kill me.

Only once more did I run into Frank Sinatra, while on a trip to Florida with girlfriends from Las Vegas. All the guys in the Rat Pack but Joey Bishop have died, as have most of the high rollers I serviced.

In a strange twist of fate, my nemesis Johnny ended up as the old man (married and otherwise) of my high-school and longtime friend Carol. Johnny's long gone, but he wasn't the last man to con me—Mafia cop Lou Eppolito took thousands to make a bogus film script of my story. He's in prison for conspiracy/murder. My ex-husband Bob drowned in the Colorado River, trying to save his adopted son.

My Grandma MoMo invited me to her home for a period during which I cared for her before her death. Long before my mother died, we talked about many things and made our peace. My brother, Dick, the only man I ever loved unconditionally, married happily—to his lovely Paula; they had three beautiful daughters. Dick died five years ago; I think of him often.

My darling daughters are happy women today. Cindy has been blessed with five children, four boys and a girl. Roberta is the mother of four sons. I am proud to be the great-grandmother of two boys. No doubt my daughters would prefer my story to be other than it is, less difficult for them and for me. But they have always tried to understand, and we are the best of friends today.

Today my life is good. I am grateful to be so many years out of the profession. I have learned many lessons—particularly to make the best of whatever life deals me.

My dreams are now twofold: to change federal and local laws regarding the sex-trade industry—that is, to make purchasing sexual services a punishable offense as is the case in Iceland and Sweden—and to build a place where prostituting women can find refuge from their pimps, put their lives in order, train for professional work paying a legitimate wage, and gain confidence and self-esteem.

Please see the resource list below and on the next page and do what you can to help!

For *The Links between Prostitution and Sex Trafficking: A Briefing Handbook*, see www.humantrafficking.org

To protest the mainstreaming of prostitution, see:
www.prostitutionresearch.com

Coalition against Trafficking in Women (CATW)
www.catwinternational.org

Look for national and local resources such as the following:
National Sexual Violence Resource Center
www.nsvrc.org

Family & Children's Service (Minnesota)
414 South Eighth Street
Minneapolis MN 55404
(612) 339-9101
www.fcsmn.org

Minnesota Coalition Against Sexual Assault (Services)
420 North Fifth Street, Suite 690
Minneapolis, MN 55401
(612) 313-2797
www.mncasa.org

For other state coalitions, see:
http://vsdvalliance.org/secGetHelp/Directory%20of%20Services/
statecoalitionssa.html

Battered Women's Justice Project
4032 Chicago Ave.
Minneapolis, MN 55407
(612) 824-8768
www.bwit.org

And the author's Web site: www.breakingmysilence.net

Index

Only the first names of the individuals following have been given, to afford privacy for them and family members surviving.

(continued)